Spirituality for Extroverts

Spirituality for Extroverts

(And Tips for Those Who Love Them)

NANCY REEVES

Abingdon Press / Nashville

SPIRITUALITY FOR EXTROVERTS
(AND TIPS FOR THOSE WHO LOVE THEM)

Copyright © 2008 by Abingdon Press

Library of Congress Cataloging-in-Publication Data

Reeves, Nancy Christine, 1952-
    Spirituality for extroverts : and tips for those who love them / Nancy Reeves.
        p. cm.
    Includes bibliographical references.
    ISBN 978-0-687-65074-3 (binding: pbk., adhesive : alk. paper)
    1. Spiritual life—Christianity.   2. Extraversion.   I. Title.

BV4509.5.R445 2008
248.4—dc22

                                                                    2007052203

08 09 10 11 12 13 14 15 16 17—10 9 8 7 6 5 4 3 2 1

MANUFACTURED IN THE UNITED STATES OF AMERICA

To Joyce Rupp, whose written and spoken words

have supported my extrovert spirituality.

I am especially grateful for her support for my own writing,

and for giving me the idea to write this book.

I am deeply grateful to the many people who have supported me

in this undertaking, especially the extroverts and introverts

who let me use their stories.

Thank you to Liz Ellmann, who sent my request for research

participants around the world on the Spiritual Directors Interna-

tional monthly email, and to my circle of spiritual friends, led by

my introvert husband, Bob, who encourage, challenge, and

comfort me on my spiritual path.

CONTENTS

INTRODUCTION

God is inexhaustibly attainable in the totality *of our action.*
—*Pierre Teilhard de Chardin*

It is a common perception that there are more extroverts than introverts in the world. Therefore you would expect many books and articles to guide extroverted persons of faith on their spiritual path. Not so! Of the thousands of spiritual guidance books lining library and bookstore shelves and described on the Internet, I could not find one that identified itself as a book on extrovert spirituality.

In fact, most spiritual guidance books encourage, solely, introvert spiritual practices such as teaching the reader to become internally quiet and shut out the world. Given this surprising state of affairs, what spiritual guidance is available to an extrovert?

Over the last twenty-eight years, I have spoken to many people about their spirituality, both in psychotherapy and spiritual accompaniment sessions. As an extrovert myself, I was sensitive to the concerns of extroverts when they told me that their ways of expressing faith were not validated or encouraged in the spiritual literature. They asked me for a book that would support their path, and I had no book to give them.

Then one day I was talking with Sister Joyce Rupp, a prolific author and workshop presenter who happens to be an introvert. Like me, Joyce had found that extroverted persons of faith frequently asked her to suggest nurturing spiritual practices that would honor their own personality. "A book needs to be written for extroverts," she stated.

Her words resonated deeply within me! When I am asking for divine guidance, I often experience an internal "door" opening and disclosing a piece of information. As I listened to Joyce, my internal door slammed open, and I felt a surge of joyous, divine energy. The message I received was, "Do it!"

I could have written a book about my own experiences, chronicling the joys and challenges of extrovert spirituality. Each of us, extrovert or introvert, has enough life stories for a large volume. But I wanted more than a personal account. So I invited folk from around the world to talk to me. In addition, I searched the history books for famous extrovert spiritual guides. I threw some psychology into the mix, along with a few of my own stories. This book is the result.

If you are an extrovert reading this book, I hope it will validate, nurture, and inspire you on your spiritual path. And if you are an introvert, I hope that you will learn to support extroverts of faith more fully, and that you may find it helpful to adopt some extroverted spiritual practices of your own.

Nancy Reeves

Part One

Getting to Know Spiritual Extroverts

1

Are You a Tigger or an Owl?

*Either we acknowledge that God is in all things or we have lost
the basis for seeing God in anything.*
—Richard Rohr

I am a retreat and workshop facilitator. For about a year, I had been having lunch at a local retreat center with a group of other facilitators and spiritual directors. We met once or twice a month and informally discussed our work, our challenges, and our joys. As I left after the fourth meeting, I became aware that I was feeling somewhat down. Although the group always welcomed me warmly at the beginning of lunch, by the end of our time together, I began noticing a cooling in our connection. I felt confused and hurt. The others all worked in the retreat center; I was an outsider. Maybe they didn't really want me there, even though they had invited me.

I expressed my hurt and confusion in prayer. And I saw, in my mind's eye, myself as the character Tigger from A. A. Milne's *Winnie the Pooh* stories. Tigger is a loveable and very bouncy tiger. "Yup, that's me," I thought. I watched myself as Tigger, bouncing into the retreat center and being greeted by a group of Owls.

When my prayer time ended, I phoned one of my friends at the retreat center and shared my experience. She laughed and said, "Tigger is a good name for you. We love having you come for lunch, but since we are all quite introverted, most of us have had enough sharing after half an hour. You're still raring to go. I start to feel overwhelmed."

I felt a wave of relief. They did like me! It was my extroverted energy that was the difficulty for my friends. Understanding our different ways of being in the world meant that subsequent lunches were much happier for all of us.

Do you view yourself more as a Tigger or an Owl? This is a book for Tiggers, although we are not always bouncy; and for Owls who want to understand and support Tiggers.

What Are Extroverts?

We extroverts are folks whose attention and energy are often directed to the outside world of people and things. We are more prone to action than contemplation. We make friends readily, adjust easily to social situations, and generally show warm interest in our surroundings.

Introverts are people whose attention and energy are more often focused on the inner world of their own thoughts and feelings. Some introverts minimize their contact with other people.

Carl Jung introduced these terms in the 1920s. They caught on and continue to be popular, because they provide a useful lens for viewing ourselves and others. [1]

Studying Extroverts' Spirituality

Once I decided to write a book on spirituality for extroverts, I wondered, "Where do I find a number of extroverts who are committed to a spiritual path and will tell me their stories?" I knew that I wanted to hear from extroverts in different countries and various faith traditions. I also wanted feedback from introverts who believe that extroverts can have a strong spiritual life.

There was no way I had time to interview even thirty people. So I decided to draw up a questionnaire and e-mail it to an initial group of people who I knew to be extroverts, even though I knew that extroverts aren't keen on this type of research tool. As Brian Shields wrote when he returned his completed form, "I would have done much better in my answers if you were to have a group of us meet and talk about this. A questionnaire is really an introvert's tool. I need to get warmed up to share better."

I hoped that the chance to tell their stories would offset the boredom of filling out the questionnaire. And it did! The topic struck a chord; responses streamed in! I received seventy-one requests for questionnaires. Carol enthused in her e-mail, "I am so excited about your research! I have read that most ministers and Christian writers (and would think almost *all* mystics) are introverts. I am an extrovert, and most of the writing just does *not* resonate with me!"

Cathie from North Carolina said, "My introverted friend forwarded me your e-mail about an extrovert research project. As I said to her, I can't believe this research is really necessary, since extroverts will tell you everything you need to know at any time anyway! But to prove my point, I would love to participate if you are still looking for folks. Because of course I would love to talk more!"

Cathie continued, "And I am particularly fascinated about 'extroverted spiritual practices.' Although I received my call to the priesthood on a five-day silent retreat, I still find quiet meditation more of a torture than a blessing (unless I am on a city bus), so I am very interested to find out how other extroverts manage their prayer life."

Other folk were interested in this topic and helped me get the word out. Liz Ellmann, Servant Leader of Spiritual Directors International, included my request in her monthly newsletter; some book publishers sent the request to their authors; I mentioned it at most of the workshops I gave; and others heard through the vast "spirituality grapevine."

The result? Fifty-eight people (fifty-one extroverts and seven introverts) completed my questionnaire. They came from the United States, Canada, New Zealand, Australia, and Peru. They ranged in age from twenty-four to eighty-eight. Over half were between fifty-four and sixty-seven years old. Seventy-six percent were female; twenty-four percent were male. Forty-four participants (seventy-six percent) were Christian, six stated they did not have a particular faith tradition, three were Jewish, two were

Unitarian Universalist, one was "interfaith," one was a Taoist, and one listed herself as a Spiritual Universalist.

The short questionnaire was designed to elicit feelings and stories. I'll be sharing many of those stories in this book, using an informal approach and tone. For those of you who want to see details about the study and its results, you'll find them at the back of this book (see Reeves Research). If you work with people in a helping capacity, these details may be helpful for you.

Extroversion—Software or Hardware?

So, when do we become extroverted? Is it part of our "hardware," or is our preferred orientation more like "software" that is dependent on our environment and society? Some recent brain research seems to indicate that extroversion is hardwired into us before birth. These studies show that different parts of the brain become more active when extroverts and introverts think in the same way. In one research project, for example, when extroverts were asked to relax and let their minds go where they wished, they tended to use the rear of their brains, the parts that receive and interpret information from the senses—in other words, they turned outward. The introverts, by contrast, were turning inward, using the front of their brains. Their brain activity was focused on the regions associated with planning, remembering, and problem solving. [2]

There are also indications that extroversion can be learned. A number of people in my study wrote of how they have become more or less extroverted over the years. When you exercise a muscle, it works more smoothly and efficiently. When you practice a musical instrument or a language, you become more proficient in it. It may be that if we consistently act in an outgoing manner, we can actually learn to be extroverted.

It appears that, as with so much about being human, the answer to our question is not solely one or the other. Extroversion is likely hardwired to some extent, and our developing personality, life experiences, family, and society have some effect as well.

When did you discover you were an extrovert? It was probably either when someone told you, or when you became aware of a difference between your own and someone else's way of being in the world. Canadian Marcia Thompson wrote, "I realized I was extroverted when I found I wanted to take leadership roles on student council."

I always knew I was more outgoing than some of my friends, but it wasn't until I took the Myers-Briggs Type Indicator (MBTI) as a university student that I had a label for my experience. I have been told numerous times, "I never really thought about my outgoing nature until I took that psychological test." At the back of the book you'll find more information on the MBTI and other common tests for extroversion.

Extroverts who learn of their orientation as children are often told by others. Eighty-two-year-old Betty Janelle, a Sister of St. Ann, was aware of her extroversion at age five! Betty wrote, "The first sentence that I remember hearing is, 'Who winds her up in the morning?' This was asked by one of my older brother's friends who was about twelve or thirteen years old."

For Sallie, a Sister of St. Joseph from Florida, it was even earlier: "I discovered that I was an extrovert as a toddler! Although I am the oldest sibling of five, I have a large extended family, and the highlight of my week was seeing all of my cousins each Sunday. Also, my folks teased me into adulthood that my first friends outside my family were the bakery man and the milkman who came to the house. I was happy to talk with them."

Twenty-four-year-old Tina wrote, "As a child I was always talking to new people, and my parents told me I was an extrovert. I can remember when I was six, I was asked to be a flower girl at a large wedding. I was so excited and couldn't wait for the rehearsal to begin. It was at an evangelical church, which was a new experience for me. Before practicing our lines and actions, the minister preached a long and fiery sermon. This was not like Sunday school where I got to talk. I sat as long as I could, then stood on the pew and called out to him, 'When do I get to talk about God?' There was a few seconds of silence, then the minister continued his sermon. My mom scooped me into her arms and explained 'the rules' in a whisper. I could see dad trying not to laugh."

Omniverts

Extroverts are more energized by interacting with the outer world; introverts with the inner world. Some folks are able to be energized by the inner world as well as the outer. They can move to the orientation that is most useful for them at any given time. I call these folk *omniverts*. The prefix *omni* means "combining all." Each omnivert will have either an extroverted or introverted inclination. Although Carl Jung did not mention omniverts, I believe he alluded to them. He talked about a "rhythmical alteration" of both extroversion and introversion as being "the normal course of life." Jung wrote that this "undisturbed flow" between the two orientations was broken by "the complicated outer conditions under which we live, as well as the presumably even more complex conditions of our individual psychic disposition." [3]

So, Jung believed that an ability to shift between being energized by the outer and inner worlds is "the normal course of life." Unfortunately, personal and societal life challenges interfere with this healthier state, and we become cut off from one of our worlds. Many people—including you, since you are reading this book—make a commitment to psychological and spiritual growth. We do what we can to work through as many personal restrictions as possible in order to heal and grow into free and loving people.

I believe that abundant life is so much more possible when we can become energized by both the inner and outer worlds. One of the goals of this book is to show how to do that. Before focusing so intensely on the topic of extroversion, I had never thought of such a thing as an omnivert. After reading the spiritual stories of so many people, however, I realized that a lot of them lived in a way that didn't match the traditional definitions of extroverts. And their personal characteristics certainly showed they weren't introverts! So, what to call them? Omnivert seemed the best fit.

You may ask, *What does an omnivert look like?* Well, on the next page you'll find an example of someone with whom I think you will be familiar.

Spiritual Role Models

Jesus of Nazareth (first century)

"I have called you friends." —John 15:15

Jesus Christ's public ministry began during a party, a wedding feast at Cana. This is a scene that extroverts can relate to. Jesus surrounded himself with followers and went out of his way to meet new people. When some complained of his inclusive and frequent socializing, Jesus replied that it was impossible to please people who held rigid expectations of how one sent from God was to behave. He compared himself to his cousin, John the Baptist: "For John came neither eating nor drinking, and they say, 'He had a demon'; the Son of Man came eating and drinking, and they say, 'Look, a glutton and a drunkard, a friend of tax collectors and sinners!' Yet wisdom is vindicated by her deeds" (Matthew 11:18-19).

Jesus taught a relational theology: God is a loving parent who wants intimacy with all people. The prayer Jesus taught begins with an assertion of the divine-human relationship. This, too, sounds like an extrovert.

And yet Jesus also drew nurturance from an introverted place. He needed time alone. Even though many would have been honored to give Jesus a bed for the night, when he was in the Jerusalem area he preferred to teach in the temple during the day and "at night he would go out and spend the night on the Mount of Olives, as it was called" (Luke 21:37). He encouraged his followers to take quiet rest time: "The apostles gathered around Jesus, and told him all that they had done and taught. He said to them, 'Come away to a deserted place all by yourselves and rest a while'" (Mark 6:30).

Jesus is a great role model of an omnivert.

What Do I Mean by Spirituality?

You are reading this book because it focuses on the spirituality of extroverts. Spirituality is something we all have. It's the way we make meaning out of life; our spirit is where our values and beliefs reside. We all have an ideal of what a good person is, even if we don't meet that ideal. Religion is a structure that some people find helps their spirituality to blossom and grow well. Others live their spirituality without this structure.

Some folk, with or without living with the structure of religion, believe in some type of higher power. They may name this power God, Spirit, Mother, Holy Mystery, Allah, Life, or many other terms. Other people on a spiritual path do not believe in a higher power. I hope this book will be helpful on your spiritual path whether you believe in a higher power or not.

I also hope the information contained in this book will help you include extroverted spiritual practices in your life, whether you are an extrovert, introvert, or omnivert. Besides information, each chapter ends with an activity to help you explore your own spirituality. In the back of the book you'll find tips on how to use this book in groups as a short course, workshop, or retreat.

Activity

The activity for this chapter is to complete the Extrovert Scale, a table I developed for my research. In the table there are spaces for you to rate yourself on qualities associated with extroverts. The qualities are listed on the left side of the table. Across the top, list the stages of your life that you would like to consider. Then fill out the remaining boxes, using the numbers 1 to 5 as indicated, to show your experience at that particular stage.

For example, you may choose to rate yourself as a young child, older child, teen, young adult, and older adult. Cythnia rated herself at the beginning of her work life and then at various times of change in her career. She found that when she was asked to take on a managerial role, she floundered for a while until she became more extroverted.

The Extrovert Scale

1 = never
2 = rarely
3 = sometimes
4 = frequently
5 = always

Outgoing—gregarious, sociable				
Comfortable in groups				
Energized by being around people				
Attention often directed outward— focusing more on people and things than on internal processes				
Like to be actively involved				
Impulsive				
Have a number of friends				
Enjoy meeting new people				

Discussion or Journal Questions

1. When did you discover you were an extrovert or an intro-vert? What were the indicators that convinced you?

2. Which three qualities, such as "outgoing" or "like to spend time alone," are strongest in you? How do these qualities help you in your life?

3. List any of these qualities that have restricted you or gotten in your way. As you continue reading this book, you will find sug-gestions for living each quality in a more helpful manner.

2
Getting Extroverts Out of the Box

As extroverts, our primary failing is to be so intimidated by introvert spirituality that we have been deprived of being able to name much of what we do as spirituality!
—*W. Paul Jones*

So, you are an extrovert. How has the experience been for you? If your extroversion has usually been validated and affirmed by others, and if you have always felt that your extrovert spirituality was a wonderful thing, you may want to skip this chapter.

If, however, your extroversion has not been honored, if you have thought of yourself as inferior to spiritual introverts, this chapter is for you. And, if you are an introvert, wanting to learn to be more supportive of the extroverts you meet on your life journey, this will be important material for you to know. I think, so often, extrovert spirituality has not been validated because it has not been understood.

In the next chapter I describe what healthy extrovert spirituality looks like. As a psychologist, however, I know that it is not enough to say, when trying to change, "I'll just let go of that restricting attitude, belief, or behavior and start to live this new, healthy one." If we have been wounded, psychologically or spiritually, we need to acknowledge and understand the wound before we can do our part in healing it.

In this chapter I will speak, briefly, of how society treats spiritual extroverts, and share a few more stories of how extroverts have been judged and misunderstood. These stories may help you remember some of your own. The purpose is not to become vengeful toward those who have wronged us. Most misunderstandings are due to ignorance.

My goal is to help you acknowledge and understand the very real restrictions you as an extrovert have encountered on your spiritual path. With that awareness, you will be able to see how you may have accepted false beliefs about your extroversion. You can then consider how to think and behave, in order to live your true spirituality. The goal of the remainder of this book is to help you do that.

How Society Views Extrovert Spirituality

Let's first look at the message society gives about extroverts and spirituality. Extroverts outnumber introverts in the world's population; estimates vary from just over fifty percent to seventy-five percent. And we are highly valued in the world at large. Focus on television or magazine ads, and you will see that successful, popular people are usually shown as gregarious—having exuberant fun with others.

The message is that extroversion equals fun and worldly success. And not just for adults. When my daughter Christina was young, she frequently dragged me in to watch television ads showing the newest toy she just *had* to own. The ads usually portrayed dolls or little ponies. I don't believe Christina would have given them another glance if the toys had been shown sitting on a shelf. What attracted my daughter was that almost every ad showed two or three little girls, each holding the toy, laughing and looking delighted. "I want that!" Christina would enthuse. "You already have some toys like that," was my invariable response. "But, look, that one is so much fun," she countered.

On the other hand, what is the message when people are shown alone in ads? (I'm excluding individuals, usually portrayed as experts or professionals, who are shown by themselves speaking to the viewer, selling a product or service.) There seem to be two basic reasons for solitary people to be portrayed in ads. The first is that they are either sick, stressed, or "losers." This type of television ad usually ends with the loser transformed, enjoying the company of friends.

The other reason solitary people are shown in ads is to indicate that they are spiritual beings. Spirituality is big business, and the ad agencies have embraced it wholeheartedly. The spiritual benefits that ads try to sell include relaxation, peace, joy, love, and harmony. It's puzzling to me how a woman, sitting in meditation in a field of daisies with a blissful expression on her face, relates to the bar of soap that is being advertised. I have yet to see an ad that includes a group of friends, relaxing over a beer, and discussing their spiritual experiences. No, spirituality is for the introvert.

Of course, we can't just blame advertisers. This image of the spiritual person as solitary and introverted may have been taken from spiritual literature. It is the rare book on spirituality that speaks positively about extroverted faith. Larry LaVelle, a United Methodist pastor, wrote, "I have come to appreciate that most devotional materials are written by and for introverts." Jo-Ann Roberts, host of a Canadian radio program, agrees: "I feel there are fewer opportunities for extroverts to grow in their spirituality. At least, that is my experience. Often when I read books on ways to improve spirituality, they suggest quiet retreat and meditation and often fail to consider those who don't find those methods all that helpful for long periods of time."

So, extroverts and introverts are both being judged and stereotyped by society. It's as if we are being put into boxes: the extrovert should be concerned with worldly success, and the introvert should be a spiritual being. This perception helps no one and harms many. It's time for those boxes to go.

Judging Extroverts

Here are some of the most common types of judgmental messages that spiritual extroverts receive. Which of them have you experienced? You may find it helpful to write your own examples in the activity at the end of this chapter.

Spiritual Guides

Sheila Pritchard

Sheila Pritchard is a New Zealander. She has been well known for many years as a spiritual director, supervisor of spiritual directors, retreat and workshop facilitator, and writer. She is the author of The Lost Art of Meditation: Deepening Your Prayer Life *and is a frequent contributor to the magazine* Closer to God. *Now self-employed, Sheila lectured for twenty years in spiritual formation at the Bible College of New Zealand.*

"Personality affects the way we live and relate to others and the way we pray. Extroverted prayer is as rich and deep as introverted prayer. When we each feel affirmed and encouraged to 'pray as we are,' we will be open to exploring and appreciating the riches of what other personality types might offer. I believe extroverts need to be affirmed in their prayer, and we need to realize that introverts often pray in extroverted ways—and vice versa. It's not about 'boxes' that fit one or the other."

"Spiritual Practices Are Done Silently, with an Inward Focus"

Extrovert writer W. Paul Jones described the message he received as he was growing up: "For over thirty years, I believed that I did not have a spiritual bone in my body.... I was born an only child in a Methodist family of two introvert parents." Jones spoke of their style of piety and spiritual practices, such as sitting "silently with our eyes tightly closed." Jones "resented shutting out all those things that truly mattered to me, as if play and friends and dogs and candy and frogs and sunsets and crunchy breakfast food had nothing to do with God." [1]

"Sharing Spiritual Experiences Is Unhealthy"

Tina Pierik, a member of the Christian Reformed Church, is part of an extroverted congregation. She grew up, however, in a denomination that was more introverted and did not encourage the sharing of spiritual experiences. So it took her some time to let go of the belief "that we extroverts are people who want to call attention to ourselves or be the center of all the action—less spiritual because we do not have a 'gentle and quiet spirit.' "

"Extroverts Have No Spiritual Depth"

Hava Kohl-Riggs, a Jewish spiritual director, told me, "I still feel inferior to introverts, that they have a stronger character and more depth. My introverted sister used to say I was a social butterfly, a shallow show-off, and her criticism still haunts me. For example, when I wrote a monthly newspaper column, I discovered I accomplished more when I worked at coffee shops. But I questioned my motives. I worried that I wrote in public only to impress people, so they'd see me writing, doing something deep. Now, I understand that, as an extrovert, when I'm working alone on a creative project, I just need to be around people to work creatively and be productive. It's not about showing off."

"Extroverts Do Not Make Effective Spiritual Guides"

Dina Gardner is a North American Presbyterian minister. She wrote, "I was one of the only extroverts in my spiritual direction training program, and I often felt like an alien from another universe. Spiritual direction communities can be very slanted toward introversion because of an often unconscious assumption that truly spiritual people are introverts. There were moments of respite from that, but animated expression, gestures, or other behaviors more typically associated with extroversion were rarely welcomed as a valid form of spiritual directing."

These judgmental messages and others like them are false. How wonderful it is that there is so much variety in this world! How boring if we were all the same! In the remainder of this book, we

Spiritual Guides

Francis Xavier (1506–1552)

Be great in little things.

As a young man in Spain, Francis was known for his gregarious nature, stylish clothes, interest in women, and social drinking. In college, he lived with three other students, one of whom was Ignatius Loyola, the founder of the Society of Jesus, whose members are known as Jesuits. At first, Francis scoffed at Ignatius's path.

Upon graduation, Francis took a post at the University of Paris. By this time, he agreed to undertake Ignatius's "spiritual exercises" program. These exercises caused his enthusiasm to shift from a focus on the world to a focus on Christ.

Francis became a Jesuit and threw himself into his new life, so much so that within nine years he burned out! Later, Ignatius appointed Francis to a missionary post in India.

Francis traveled extensively in Asia, baptizing, preaching, and teaching to thousands. He learned Tamil so he could speak directly to the people of Ceylon, where he was popular with children as well as adults. He translated Christian scripture and prayers into their language, and composed and sang simple rhymes to make learning easier and more enjoyable. Francis's adaptability helped him connect to others.

He kept in contact with his brother Jesuits in Europe, writing, "Let me tell you what I have done so that I may never forget you. For my own great comfort and that I may have you constantly in mind, I have cut from your letters to me your names written in your own hand, and these I always carry about with me, together with the vow of profession which I made, to be my solace and refreshment."[2]

will explore how we extroverts can live our spirituality openly and joyously. I'm also extending the invitation for introverts to try some of the extroverted spiritual practices I describe. When someone tries to convert an extrovert to be an introvert, or vice versa, it diminishes both parties. Let's help each other get out of our boxes!

Activities

Getting Out of the Box (for Extroverts and Introverts)

Choose a few advertisements from magazines or television that use spirituality to sell their product. Explore what they say about extroversion. (If the exercise is done in a group, many more insights will be generated.) Now write your own ads, showing extroverts as spiritual. Be playful; don't worry about the explicit materialism at this point.

Personal History (for Extroverts)

Draw a timeline from your birth to the present. Remember significant experiences in your life, looking specifically for evidence of your extroversion. Mark these on the timeline. It can be interesting to compare notes with others who are doing the same exercise. After you have your timeline completed, answer one or more of the following questions.

1. When did you first become aware of your extroversion?
2. What words would you use to describe how you perceived your extroversion?
3. What words have others used to describe your extroversion?
4. What judgments or false beliefs did you encounter about your extroversion?
5. How did your extroversion and your spirituality interact? For example, one participant said it made her more willing to ask others about their beliefs.

Discussion or Journal Questions

1. In the past, what was your perception of extrovert and introvert spirituality? For example, did you view extroverts as better at social justice or introverts as deeper?

2. Have you had an experience of being judged or put in a box? Please describe it.

3. Francis Xavier had the experience of being burned out as he enthusiastically embraced his lifework. Have you had this experience? How have you learned to balance or limit your extroversion?

3
What Does Extrovert Spirituality Look Like?

I live my life in widening circles
that reach out across the world.
—*Rainer Maria Rilke*

Qualities of Extrovert Spirituality

So, what does extrovert spirituality look like? One way to answer the question is to discuss the qualities that are listed in the Extrovert Scale found at the end of chapter 1, giving some examples of how each quality can contribute to our spirituality. The only one of these qualities I won't be discussing in this chapter is "impulsive." I will be talking about impulsiveness in chapter 12, "Challenges of Being Extroverted Persons of Faith."

As you read the list of qualities below, keep in mind that every extrovert is different, and you will invariably find yourself relating to some of these qualities more than to others. We each have our own unique personalities, skills, challenges, and life experiences that shape us. Also, our families, communities, society, culture, and religion have influenced our ways of being in the world. After all, even Tigger was not bouncy all the time, and as he continued to live with the other animals in the Hundred Acre Wood he learned to respond to life in many other ways.

Extrovert spirituality tends to be:

Outgoing

Sociable, gregarious, friendly—all these synonyms for *outgoing* describe the psychologically and spiritually healthy extrovert. When we are outgoing, we tend to be more visible to others. They will not only become aware of our personality more quickly than they would with an introvert; they will learn anything we wish to share. We extroverts share what interests us. So, if spirituality is important in our lives, others will hear about it. Grania Radcliffe, a Roman Catholic woman, told me, "My extroversion helped me not be afraid to show my love of God."

One benefit of being outgoing with our spirituality is that we attract others who hold similar beliefs. This encourages the growth of spiritual friendships, which can support, guide, and challenge us on our path. Canadian Linda Leone found that her outgoing personality helped her spiritual life blossom: "By speaking up, starting conversations, sharing about myself, and listening to others share their stories, I have found spiritual practices that are meaningful to me."

The visibility of extrovert spirituality may also be beneficial to others. Richard Morgan is an extrovert and prolific author of books in the area of spirituality, aging, and pastoral care. He wrote, "I especially have observed how shy, withdrawn people 'open up' and share their life stories when I take the initiative to be outgoing and extroverted with them."

Comfortable in Groups

We can worship alone, and we can worship with others. Extrovert spirituality tends more to worshiping in groups, as long as our spirituality is accepted. That doesn't mean extroverts never pray alone. Of course we do. As I describe in a later chapter, however, solitary worship in extroverts often has a relational aspect.

Sometimes the fact that we tend to be comfortable in groups encourages us to join faith communities. Singer, songwriter, and musical animator Linnea Good wrote that her extroversion has "made me a churchgoer. Even though the church worship often does not fill much of my spiritual longing, I draw strength and a sense of greater-than-the-sum-of-our-parts with others. When it comes to music *and* performance, this is the point. It has given me mentors and role models; it has made a collaborator out of me despite my reticence to share."

Marion, an extroverted artist, also found that her comfort in groups influenced her spiritual path: "I think it brought me to the church in the first place—I enjoy being with others who have similar interests. I like working in a collaborative way with others."

Energized by Being Around People

Introverts tend to be drained after a time of interacting with others; extroverts come out of the same contact energized. I had an "extrovert experience" a few weeks ago when I had just recovered from viral meningitis. I was still pretty weak, so asked my husband, Bob, to come with me as driver and helper during a daylong workshop for the local Hospice Society. Bob was there so that if I needed to lie down, for example, he could take over and form the participants into small groups. I had prepared some questions if needed.

The organizer was concerned about me. She told me later that I looked pale and shaky—that is, until I started speaking. Bob, who was watching me closely, said that within a few minutes my color changed and I sounded stronger than I had in weeks. He compared it to a drooping flower being watered. I remember looking at all the interested faces gazing back at me and feeling a flow of energy. I not only sounded stronger than I had in weeks, I felt stronger. This experience was a powerful example of how extroverts are energized by being around others.

How does the energy play out in extrovert spirituality? When we experience something as life-giving, we want more of it. So, when we make a commitment to walking a spiritual path, we will be drawn to spiritual practices that involve others. Wade Lifton, a youth leader in Vancouver, wrote, "I find that the presence of other people helps focus spiritual practices for me. I am often easily distracted when I am alone."

Some extroverts are aware of more than just "people energy" when they are around others. Many extroverts have said something similar to Cathie Caimano, an Episcopal priest from North Carolina: "I definitely feel God's presence when I am with a lot of other people. I imagine this has something to do with my becoming a priest."

Attention Often Directed Outward

At first glance, this quality may seem identical to the one labeled "outgoing." Actually, they can be quite different. People whose attention is directed outward aren't always interested in interaction. To put it another way, I can find that my attention is focused on the outer world, the world of people and things, and yet not want to interact much with that world.

Since extroverts enjoy directing their attention to the outside world, we tend to look there for spiritual meaning. Debra Faulk is a Unitarian Universalist minister from Toronto. She wrote, "I witness the sacred in everything; the whole of creation is holy. I can see the external beauty reflected within as well. Perhaps my outward orientation has opened me to this quality of seeing the sacred everywhere."

Like to Be Actively Involved

Unless an extrovert has low self-esteem or some other psychological wound, we tend not to be wallflowers. We want to participate rather than just watch. Seventy-three-year-old Sister Vanessa says about her spirituality, "I'm a doer," as she describes her busy life. Extroverts are likely to take courses, volunteer for good causes, and be attracted to worship services where we feel our outgoing energy is welcome. When I ask for feedback after conducting a workshop, the extroverts often say, "It would have been great to have more small groups," while the introverts suggest more individual quiet time for reflection.

Linda Leone explains one way that she is actively involved in her church: "I am a Eucharistic Minister; I stand beside the priest, and people receive communion from me. I was asked to do this, and after my first time sharing the host I had a vision of sorts. I was like a prism, and the light of Christ was shining from me to others as I passed out the host or gave the wine. I enjoy this ministry immensely. As I get to know people, I use their names as I share the body of our Lord. I like to be personal. I enjoy people, and this joy brings me closer to God."

A number of extroverts over the years have told me that one of their favorite spiritual practices is to volunteer or find other ways to be of service to others. Singer-songwriter Linnea Good reserves a portion of her time to provide music to groups who could not afford her services. She adds that her extroversion "has also made me a social-activist Christian. I see my life as one continuous spiritual practice and the Spirit as constantly and without cease sending messages of love and guidance."

There is another aspect of extrovert spirituality that fits in this section. Extroverts tend to participate in a large number of spiritual practices. Nearly half the extroverts I spoke with said they currently use six or more different spiritual practices. Eight extroverts told me they had ten or more regular spiritual practices, and one listed twenty-four! When I shared this information with one of my introvert friends, the response was, "Goodness, I couldn't keep track of them all."

This is a lot of active involvement! Although more spiritual practices are not necessarily better, we extroverts, with our love of variety, are drawn to a greater number of spiritual practices than are introverts. Some of the biological research seems to indicate that our brains need more stimulation than those of introverts. Extrovert spiritual director and writer Kathleen Finley told me she began collecting different ways to pray, which resulted in her book *Savoring God: Praying with All Our Senses.* In it she discusses how to pray with more than thirty daily objects.

Have a Number of Friends

"My extrovertedness has kept me rooted in spiritual community instead of becoming a holy hermit," Wade Lifton wrote. Having a number of friends, and being interested in sharing spiritual experiences, means the extrovert is more likely to hear a number of different beliefs, stories, and viewpoints.

Just over ten years ago, God spoke to me in prayer and invited me into a more intimate, intentional relationship. I was blown away! One of the many consequences of that experience was my sudden interest in learning more about my Christian path. So I asked my friends questions and sought out stories of their spiritual experiences. I bought a Bible concordance and explored some of the themes I was particularly interested in, such as God's love for us and desire to be in relationship.

A few months later, I was in a group of people at coffee time after the Sunday service. A friend, who had been away for some months, listened to our conversation for a bit, then said, "Nancy, it sounds like you've just taken a course in Christian spirituality. You're talking about concepts I know you weren't familiar with before I left. How did you learn so much so quickly?" I thought for a moment, then noticed my friends grinning and rolling their eyes. I replied, "When I'm interested in something, I ask questions. Now I'm passionately interested in Christianity, and my friends have been so gracious in answering all my queries."

Having a number of friends also means more opportunities to be invited to spiritual gatherings or other activities. When a new speaker comes to town, I am likely to hear about it from a few friends before I read about it in the newspaper.

Enjoy Meeting New People

In order to grow spiritually or psychologically, we need to be willing to embrace newness. This newness can come as ideas, experiences, feelings, or sensations. We extroverts enjoy meeting strangers, who introduce us to new ways of being spiritual. Justin related that he is always striking up conversations with strangers on buses and airplanes. If they seem to be of another religion, he asks questions about their faith. He told me, "I've had some deeply meaningful sharings. These conversations have helped me articulate and more fully explore my own spiritual path."

Another benefit of meeting new people is that the more we

meet, the more likely we are to find folks with whom we wish to develop deeper spiritual friendships. In any large group, there may be only a few others whose spirituality seems so compatible with mine that I wish more intimacy. One woman spoke of her extroverted impulse to be visible in her spirituality and how this impulse combined with her interest in meeting new people: "What you see is what you get. I meet a lot of people who can accept my beliefs, because people who don't agree tend to avoid me. It means relationships can reach a deeper stage more quickly."

With our comfort and interest in meeting new people, spiritual extroverts are more likely to volunteer for service that involves interacting with others. Generally we find it appealing to help people both by getting to know a few on a deep level and caring for large groups of strangers.

The Spiritual Extrovert

In sum, spiritual extroverts tend to be friendly people who initiate conversation. If you show any interest in spirituality, they will share their own beliefs and might tell you some of their experiences. They will also be interested in hearing yours. You will find that they are very responsive to the outer world, and in fact see evidence of God's presence in many ways. They have a number of spiritual practices and actively participate in the groups or spiritual communities to which they belong.

Spiritual Role Models

Gabrielle Bossis (1874–1950)

Hunt for me everywhere: I will let myself be caught with such joy! How did you expect to find me if you didn't search? As soon as you have found me, give me to others; there are people I am waiting to reach only through you.[1]

As a young child in France, Gabrielle began to hear an inner voice who identified himself as Jesus. Gabrielle wanted to believe, yet it took her some years to be convinced the voice was indeed Christ. Shy as a child, Gabrielle matured into a strong extrovert. She became a well-known author of spiritual comedies. Gabrielle began to act in her comedies, and her career as an actress took off. She was feted, honored, and loved by many in numerous countries.

Throughout her busy social life, Gabrielle's spirituality grew. At one point her spiritual director suggested she join a convent. Jesus, speaking within her, told her how delighted he was with her acting, which gave her a rich spiritual life and an enjoyable outward life of travel, friends, and work.

At age sixty-two, her inner voice spoke so frequently that Gabrielle carried on an almost continual dialogue with Christ. She began to write these conversations in a diary, which was published as *Lui et Moi* ("He and I"). The popular book was subsequently translated into English. In a biography of Gabrielle Bossis, Jose de Vink writes, "The extraordinary example Gabrielle Bossis managed to give on how to successfully lead a twofold life—temporal and spiritual."[2]

Gabrille wrote that Jesus frequently told her how much we are loved, that God longs for us to ask for a deeper relationship and enjoys living within a person who is aware of the divine internal presence. The interaction of Gabrielle Bossis's extroversion and spirituality bore nourishing fruit.

God for Extroverts

*At a certain stage in the path of devotion,
the devotee finds satisfaction in God with form,
and at another stage, in God without it.*
—Ramakrishna Parmahansa (1836–1886)

Out of the limitless images or ways of experiencing an infinite God, we all have our favorites. These favorites support and nurture our spirituality. We also may have images from our past that frighten or otherwise restrict us. For example, many people have been told by someone in their early lives that God is a punitive deity. If they develop a relationship with this God, it is one based on fear of punishment.

Healthy spirituality is a process of examining our beliefs about the divine, nurturing those that help us achieve freedom and abundant life, and healing or letting go of the beliefs that restrict and diminish us. With maturing spirituality, the way we experience the divine-human relationship also changes, becoming more life-enhancing. Ways of relating to and experiencing God expand and deepen. Paul Hawker, an extroverted author from New Zealand, described his divine-human relationship as "evolving, ever changing, and sometimes, when I can get enough of me out of the way, achingly beautiful."

Who is God for extroverts? Here are some of our favorite images and experiences.

God as Relationship

Many extroverts speak of God as a being with whom we are in relationship. This is not a surprise, since extroverts put so much emphasis on interacting with others. Some divine images I have heard of are: Father, Mother, Jesus, Holy Spirit, a Wise Woman, a Loving Parent. Martha wrote, "I see God as a close friend/lover/parent, more intimate with the deepest part of me than I am with myself. It is a relationship with Mystery which can take many forms."

God as Energy

Another very common experience of God for extroverts is as energy. Sherry Gaugler, a spiritual director from Minneapolis, wrote, "I see God in the form of energy and light and love. I experience God in many ways—He continues to surprise me."

Martin from Victoria spoke of a "flow of Being," and Bob from Detroit described "hugeness, awesome everythingness, with me a teeny-infinitessimal but real part." Franciscan Sister Marj English experienced an energy with "an ebb and flow to it," and Episcopalian Roz Malone wrote, "When I am in prayer or deeper meditation it is this diffused energy that I feel connected with—a sense of floating in a vast interconnected pool of spirit energy."

God as Sensation or Felt Quality

For some extroverts God is more a physical sensation or a felt quality. This experience of the Holy is still a relational one. Brenda, a Catholic, wrote, "It fills and knows me and wants to move all of us toward more love." Other words and phrases to describe God in this way included: "love like a raging ocean," "constant, peaceful Presence," "divine presence and spirit," "a feeling, a bodily experience of open presence, connecting."

One respondent described "a very warm feeling in my solar plexus which radiates from the center out, down my arms. It is a wonderful, nourishing feeling. My thinking is suspended. My experience of God is physical rather than mental."

God with Skin On

Some extroverts are keenly aware of God's presence in family, friends, acquaintances, members of their community, and strangers. There is a story circulating in spiritual circles that may not actually have happened and yet in some sense is true:

Fred, an old man who lived on the street, frequented an inner-city soup kitchen. He was loud, he stank of alcohol, and he was rude to everyone who spoke to him. Only Joe, one of the volunteers, persevered in attempts to have a conversation with him. Eventually Fred was found unconscious in a dark alley. He was taken to hospital, and it became obvious that Fred was close to death. As his life ebbed away, a hospital chaplain approached and told Fred that he would soon be meeting God. "Would you like to meet God?" the chaplain asked the dying man. "Only if God is like Joe," was the weak response.

Your God

Who or what is God for you? One of the activities at the end of this chapter explores this question. I believe the more images and experiences we can associate with our Creator, the deeper and broader the relationship will be.

Divine Guidance for Extroverts

I define spiritual discernment as tuning in to divine guidance for the small and large decisions in our lives. Spiritual discernment is listening for and acting on the "still, small voice" that Oprah refers to on her website. Some people think of spiritual discernment as a method, such as prayer, to use when we have a concern or decision to make. Over the past eight years I have done research on discernment in a number of faith traditions, and I believe it is more productively viewed as an attitude. If we cultivate the attitude of discernment, we will be ready whenever that still, small voice speaks.

What my experience and research tell me is that inspiration can and may come when we least expect it—and in ways we could never have anticipated! We may receive guidance through our least favored quality or inclination, since a goal of the Divine Guide is to encourage wholeness. For example, I encourage extroverts to nurture some qualities of introvert spirituality, because God may choose to speak to them in quiet ways; just as introverts can benefit by developing some qualities of extrovert spirituality, because God may come to them through the outside world.

One important way in which God communicates with us in the outside world is through people. Some people may be unintentional prophets who don't realize they are speaking words of

---

Spiritual Guides

Oprah Winfrey (1954–)

What I've learned is that when I don't know what to do, do nothing. Sit still and listen for that small voice that will always lead you and guide you. If you're quiet and listen, you will hear it.[3]

Oprah Winfrey was born January 29, 1954, in rural Mississippi. A graduate of Tennessee State University, she is considered the most powerful woman in entertainment. Head of a huge media company, including television and magazines, she is known for her active compassion to those in need and for her strong interest in spirituality. In an interview she said, "The responsibility of people who have money and fame and some kind of clout is to use that in a meaningful way."

Check out Oprah's website, www.oprah.com. It is chockfull of spirituality. There are articles and interviews to teach the reader to meditate, including a journal Oprah wrote when she made a three-day retreat. The website also includes spiritual thoughts for the day, stories of inspiring people, and other articles of a spiritual nature.

---

wisdom for us. Others may be aware that they are a channel for the divine. Sometimes the people are strangers or acquaintances, but most of the time they are likely to be family, friends, or those we seek out to talk about our spirituality. Sister Vanessa, the "doer" whom we met earlier, wrote, "I'm a people person. My divine guidance comes in daily living most of the time. Events and people in my life have directed me on the way."

James Harnish, a United Methodist pastor and author from Tampa, Florida, told me how God had guided him through a very confusing period of his life by making use of his extroverted qual-

42

ities: "It was a time of intense tension and transition in the life of the congregation I serve. There were times when the primary way in which I sensed the guidance of the Holy Spirit was through the response, correction, or support I received from other people. First, there were the people in the congregation who were a constant sounding board for my anxieties and concerns. My extroverted way of working through the problem was to talk about it with them and receive their guidance. Second, I was in a small group with three other pastors who met regularly for mutual sharing, support, and prayer. Through their feedback and guidance, I found clarity about my role in leadership and the direction I should take. I'm convinced that I never would have experienced the sense of God's guidance in my life if I had tried to find it inside myself."

Lots of people will give you advice or suggestions that come from their own thoughts and feelings. Their sharing may or may not be useful. Every so often, though, we hear words that touch us very deeply. We know this guidance is God speaking through the other. In my book *A Match Made in Heaven* I give an example of how one person experiences this inner knowing.

Sandra has a gift for listening to people, which is one reason she is such a popular high school teacher. She realized some years ago that she often receives God's messages through "unintentional prophets" she meets on the bus riding to work. Sandra strikes up many conversations with strangers and often is given advice. In most cases, she knows the suggestions are of human origin.

Every so often, however, Sandra hears words that seem to "tingle" within her. She explains, "When this happens, I know that person is being a vessel for the Spirit. They usually don't realize this, although once an older man paused and said, 'That didn't come from me. Do you believe in God?' When I told him I did, he continued, 'Well, I don't know what those words meant for you, but I do know we've both just been blessed with the Spirit's presence.' We smiled at each other and sat in grateful silence until my stop came." [4]

Hearing divine wisdom from others directly is one type of spiritual discernment. Another involves intentionally taking in information in a setting that is comfortable for the extrovert personality. For example, although extroverts can and do read (after all, you're reading this book!), we benefit by having a place to discuss and process what we learn from books.

Some studies show that extroverts are much more likely than introverts to attend workshops, courses, and other venues that encourage discussion and activities. Larry LaVelle emailed a few days after sending in his completed questionnaire. He wrote, "Answering your questionnaire got me thinking.... Walking home this morning from my coffee group, it dawned on me that I have made use of educational experiences during critical or major transitions—for example, college as a break from my small hometown in Iowa; seminary as the beginning of my future life as a minister; Doctor of Ministry during midlife transition; a thirty-day Ignatian retreat where I discovered (from out of nowhere, it seemed) that I wanted out of ministry, a covenant I had made even before my marriage vows. It all worked out when I was appointed to what became my last church, and loved it."

Spiritual discernment is a gift from God. Divine guidance is about showing us how to be the free, loving people we were meant to be. For extroverts, as my respondents have shown, some of the best sources of divine guidance are people: those we know and trust, groups with similar interests and goals, and even strangers.

In part 2, we will explore specific extroverted spiritual practices that encourage a deepening relationship with the divine. Before you read it, however, take some time to complete one or more of the following activities.

CR====V====O

Activities

Your Extrovert Spirituality (for Extroverts)

Now that you've seen how the extroverted qualities of some others reflect and shape their spirituality, here's a chance for you to explore your own extroverted faith. Answer the question below for each item listed, recording examples from your own life. You will probably need a journal or diary in which to write your answers. Talking with others may remind you of some of your own past experiences. You may find it helpful to take several days or even longer with this activity, as memories may continue to surface for some time.

How do the following interact with your spirituality?

- Outgoing
- Comfortable in groups
- Energized by being around people
- Attention often directed outward
- Like to be actively involved
- Have a number of friends
- Enjoy meeting new people

Who Is God for You? (for Extroverts and Introverts)

Write, draw, or discuss ways in which your image or experience of God (or whatever term fits for you) has changed or stayed the same over your lifetime. How did your own image or experience compare with the ones that were taught to you?

Discussion or Journal Questions

1. Discuss a time when you received divine guidance through another person. Did you seek out this guidance, or did it come out of the blue?

2. Have you learned something new about the qualities of extroverts through this chapter? If so, what?

3. How do you perceive God (or whatever term fits for you) in your life at the present time?

Part Two

Extrovert
Spiritual Practices

4
A Few Words about Spiritual Practice

God will give you the building blocks
but God cannot build your spiritual house for you.
—R. Grace Imathiu

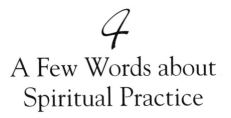hen many people think about spiritual practice, sitting prayer is what comes to mind. Spiritual practice is really much broader than that. Any intentional activity that turns our awareness more fully to the divine is a spiritual practice. And any activity can have a spiritual component, as you will see in the following chapters.

Any spiritual practice can be done in an extroverted or introverted way. Some extroverts follow the inclination most familiar to them and do spiritual practices in an extroverted manner. Others say that spiritual practice is a time for them to be open to more introverted energy. James Harnish wrote, "Spiritual disciplines are where my introvert scale kicks in. I really appreciate quiet, meditative prayer and reflection on Scripture. I am at home in meditative small groups."

Many other extroverts say they do some extroverted and some introverted practices. Diane Jorgensen is a spiritual director from Nebraska. She commented, "As I grow older I find that extroverted and introverted practices are very intertwined. All of these practices keep me both centered and energized. When I don't do any practices I get stuck, stagnate, and feel dead inside, and the energy drains out of me, and I get depressed."

Richard Morgan wrote, "I believe spirituality is both inward and outward. Spiritual reading and meditation are spiritual practices most helpful, as is daily journal writing. Being alone with God is crucial. As an older person, aging is a love affair with God. But I also believe spirituality is found in involvement with people. I am increasingly becoming aware of the spirituality of people with Alzheimer's and dementia. Although their bodies and minds may be gone, their souls are alive, and in my ministry with them I dis- cover the presence of God."

In the following chapters I will briefly describe the seven most common spiritual practices mentioned by the people who an- swered my questionnaire. Of course, there are many more. Dr. Pa- tricia Brown, an associate professor of spiritual formation and direction at Mars Hills Graduate School in Seattle, was speaking about prayer, but could have been talking more generally about spiritual practices, when she wrote in her book *Paths to Prayer*, "There are as many ways to pray as there are souls who walk the earth." [1]

Discussion or Journal Questions

1. What are your favorite spiritual practices? How has your spir- ituality changed because of practicing them?

2. Choose one of your spiritual practices. Would you identify it with extroversion or introversion? What would it look like if you practiced it with the opposite orientation?

5
Praying and Meditating

Have you given flight to the dreams that you keep?
Have you touched the underground streams of the deep?
Come, give your imaginings birth.
—Linnea Good, songwriter and omnivert

There are many ways to pray and meditate, and before I talk about some of them, let's look at definitions. *Prayer* is simply communication with the divine. Sometimes we are aware that the communication flow is from us to God. This we may call active prayer. Sometimes we may listen for a message or other touch from the Spirit. This is listening or contemplative prayer. In this chapter, the focus is on prayer that is done in one physical position. I call it sitting prayer, although some folks prefer to lie or kneel or stand throughout their prayer time. Later chapters will look at prayer in movement.

The word *meditation* carries a different meaning to folks in Eastern and Christian faith traditions. In the East, meditation is akin to Christian contemplative or listening prayer. In the Christian tradition, to meditate usually means to think about something, such as a Scripture passage, deeply and carefully. I will refer to both meanings in this chapter.

Active Prayer

My parents didn't go to church or let me go when I asked for permission. In fact, they told me to stay away from God, who

51

tended to kill babies (such as my brother) and make life difficult for believers. In spite of or maybe because of this belief, my parents made me say a conciliatory prayer before bed as insurance, in case I didn't make it through the night. However, I had had some experiences lying in bed after they left that showed me a very different deity than the cruel, vengeful one they believed in. So my nightly prayer, instead of being recited with fear, was said with love:

> Now I lay me down to sleep
> I pray the Lord my soul to keep.
> If I should die before I wake
> I pray the Lord my soul to take.

Active prayers may be learned, or created by the person praying. They may be prescribed for certain situations or times of day, such as the prayer known as grace that is usually spoken before a meal, or a prayer of thanksgiving or petition. Worship services usually contain a mixture of active prayers that are said every time, and other prayers for certain times of the year. Active prayer can be done in an extroverted or introverted manner, depending on the direction of our focus.

Contemplative Prayer or Meditation

Many of my respondents reported that they practiced contemplative prayer or meditation. As they described their experiences to me, I realized they were talking about two types: extroverted and introverted. Strange as it may seem, most of the written guides to contemplative prayer and meditation only describe the introverted type. In fact, some people shared experiences of extroverted contemplative prayer with an addendum such as: "I'm probably praying wrong," "I know this isn't the way it's supposed to be done," "I don't really tell my spiritual director what I'm doing," or "Spiritual practice? Well, I do a kind of contemplative prayer, but not the one the books talk about."

Introverted Contemplative Prayer

In what I now call introverted contemplative prayer, the person praying or meditating uses something such as a short word, a mantra, or the act of breathing to focus the attention. If thoughts, feelings, or sensations from within or without are experienced, the person does not respond. If the mind wanders to something other than the focus, it is gently brought back as soon as the person realizes what has happened. Examples of this introverted spiritual practice include the various types of Eastern meditation, Vipassana, Transcendental Meditation, Christian Centering Prayer, and Christian Meditation.

Extroverted Contemplative Prayer

In extroverted contemplative prayer or meditation, a focus such as those described above may be used, or the person may sit in silence with a wordless longing for connection with God. Thoughts and feelings that originate within the individual are disregarded. When a "divine touch" occurs, however, the person responds. Some of these touches are described as "unconditional love," "delight," "an embrace," "the physical sensation of intelligent electricity," and "an awareness of a call or solution to a problem." The experience of extroverted contemplative prayer can also involve sensations described as "seeing a Light that evokes wonder and awe in me," "a quiet resting, like I'm floating on water," and "an awareness of loving Presence."

When these experiences occur, the person praying responds. Usually the response is an outpouring of love, gratitude, awe, or a relinquishing of worry or pain. If at any time the person becomes aware of thinking about the experience rather than being with it, the focus is returned to a longing for connection. For example, if a problem has been presented and a divine solution received, the person praying would not spend time at that moment sorting it out. That is for later. During prayer time the solution is accepted with gratitude, and the attention remains on the divine-human relationship.

Here is what some folks said about their extroverted contemplative prayer:

John Oldham, a hymn writer from Winnipeg, wrote, "Sometimes I do walking meditation, and sometimes sitting. I wait silently, receptive to divine energy. As I experience it, I am engaged, and there is an interaction with that divine energy. The engagement draws me in. I am absorbed into the force field. My response is wonder and awe. Sometimes I feel I am in a state of rapture for some time."

Leslie Black, a holistic therapist and educator from Victoria, reported, "I want to be fully present when taking intentional time to be with God, so I always start my prayer time by grounding myself in my body and then opening my heart center to connect with the Light of Christ within. I am then often quickly transported into a deep silence where I experience living and peaceful connection with the Holy One. And my heart opens more and more through this connection."

Myself, I start my prayer with the words or just the intent, "Pray me as you wish me prayed." Then I wait, with longing and in surrender. Sometimes I have the sense that God wishes me to do some type of introvert prayer practice. More frequently I move into the extroverted type. The whole prayer may just be a time of waiting. If I am distracted, I gently bring my focus back to my intent.

I have been doing this for years, and have experienced God in so many different ways. Once, I "saw" a delightful, swirling, playful energy. I felt a strong invitation to enter the dance. So I said yes, and there was a long time of moving together, during which I lost most of my sense of self. I came out of that prayer time refreshed and then realized that I had been too serious about a situation in my life. After the prayer I could see it in perspective. I have also experienced introverted prayer as a guiding, comforting, faith-deepening time.

Origins of Christian Contemplative Prayer

The fifteenth-century book *The Cloud of Unknowing* provided a foundation for introverted Christian contemplative prayer. In it, the anonymous author describes using a short word as a prayer focus. An introverted Lutheran pastor I know pointed out to me that the same book also encourages an extroverted practice: entering the prayer "with a loving stirring and a blind beholding unto the naked being of God Himself only." [1]

As described in the book, the "cloud of unknowing" is what keeps us from experiencing God's presence. The author advises the person praying:

> Lift up thy love to that cloud: rather, if I shall say thee sooth, let God draw thy love up to that cloud and strive thou through help of His grace to forget all other thing.... Then will He sometimes peradventure send out a beam of ghostly light, piercing this cloud of unknowing that is betwixt thee and Him; and shew thee some of His privity, the which man may not, nor cannot speak. Then shalt thou feel thine affection inflamed with the fire of His love, far more than I can tell thee, or may or will at this time. [2]

This description sounds like the experience of many people who practice extroverted contemplative prayer. Both introverted and extroverted contemplative prayer are examples of what is called apophatic contemplation. Thomas Keating, the foremost proponent of centering prayer, defines apophatic contemplation as "resting in God beyond the exercise of particular acts, except to maintain a general loving attention to the divine presence." [3]

Extroverted or Introverted Prayer?

Is extroverted or introverted prayer best? Some extroverts practice introverted contemplative prayer alone. Others prefer to do the introverted practice with a group, either to be part of the accumulated energy or to have the chance to talk afterward. Some of my respondents reported that they only practice extroverted contemplative prayer, and some pray both types. Which is best for you? I believe that, if you are receptive, God will guide you to the type of practice that will meet your needs and life circumstances.

Spiritual Guides

Wilkie Au

Wilkie Au is a professor of theological studies at Loyola Mary-mount University in Los Angeles. He is the author of the award-winning books, By Way of the Heart: Toward a Holistic Spirituality *and* The Enduring Heart: Spirituality for the Long Haul. *With Noreen Cannon Au, he has written* Urgings of the Heart *and* The Discerning Heart: Exploring the Christian Path, *which was awarded first place in the category of Pastoral Ministry by the Catholic Press Association of the United States and Canada in 2007. He teaches in the area of Christian spirituality and has been a spiritual director for many years. He is also an extrovert.*

"When people describe the results of their extroverted contemplative prayer as 'an outpouring of love, gratitude, awe, and surrender,' they are clearly being touched by the Spirit of God. Any prayer form that results in the fruit of the Spirit as noted by St. Paul (Galatians 5:22-24), qualifies as authentic prayer. Methods of prayer, whether oriented in an introverted or extroverted way, are merely means to being in communion with God. Prayer forms are meant to be instrumental. When they help us attain what we desire, we should not let them occupy our attention. As an ancient Chinese proverb states, 'Only the fool stares at the finger, when it is pointing to the moon.'"

Extroverted contemplative prayer takes as much discipline as does the introverted type. Staying with a wordless longing for divine connection can be difficult. Thoughts intrude, boredom rears its ugly head, and our ego can manufacture experiences that appear to be from God. Divine touches are not guaranteed for every prayer session.

After I had read a number of examples of extroverted contemplative prayer, I sent descriptions back to my research participants who had only indicated that they practiced prayer or meditation. Which of these do you do? I asked them. It turned out the majority practiced extroverted prayer. Some did both. Here are two responses I received to my question:

Wade Lifton wrote:

> Nancy, your words so accurately describe my experience of meditation, in a way that I've never been able to articulate. What you describe as introverted contemplative prayer is often what I try to do. Your description of extroverted contemplative prayer really accurately describes my actual experience: the longing for connection with the Holy, and the feelings of overwhelming gratitude, joy, and peace when I experience that connection.
>
> Sometimes I worry that I'm focusing on a result by trying to achieve that state of gratitude, joy, and peace. But I remind myself that my focus is to open myself to the Holy, not to achieve a state of being, and that the Holy is always waiting to share that connection.
>
> I notice that my belly is the place where I carry tension, anxiety, and where I close myself off. When I connect with the Holy through stillness and quiet I feel energy or light in my belly, melting away tension, opening my being. I feel my deepest power, my truest self, my connection with the Holy channeling out of my belly into the world.

Brenda, a spiritual director, wrote, "I am excited to read this! It is a description of the moments I define as my deepest prayer—referring, of course, to the extroverted contemplative prayer or meditation! I am familiar with the introverted style. I use it for myself and use that kind of description when I am leading a group into a guided meditation experience. But the *longing* you describe, the reaching out to connect with Presence, is a very fundamental aspect of my spirituality. I am always very grateful when I enter this type of experience. It seems to happen more easily at this stage of my life, but my gratitude is as full and stunned as the first time I felt it. 'Being with,' 'longing for connection,' and 'feeling connected' are all part of those moments."

Spiritual Guides

Carol A. Fournier

Carol A. Fournier is the cofounder and director of the Silver Dove Institute, an educational nonprofit center in Vermont. The institute is dedicated to supporting interfaith dialog as well as providing training in spiritual guidance for individuals and the community. Carol is a spiritual guide and nationally certified counselor who specializes in spiritual development, ethics, and counseling. She offers spiritual guidance, retreats, and programs internationally.

"Reading the beautiful sharings of so many individuals committed to a living journey of intimacy and tenderness with God was touching and humbling.

I noticed in the sharings how difficult it is to find words for the deepest and most intimate experiences of the Divine. Regardless of how the experience of contemplation was described, either extroverted or interoverted, both bore fruit in service to the unfoldment of guidance, faith, and a love of God.

As an interfaith spiritual director, I have observed over the past fifteen years that an individual's commitment to spiritual practice, in this case contemplative prayer, is essential to the effectiveness of the practice in supporting an ever-deepening relationship with God. This is combined with the willingness to trust, let go, and surrender to the enduring and mysterious presence of God.

Ultimately the burning question I feel in my heart in response to these sharings is, 'How did you grow in love through your experience?' In the end, regardless of the contemplative experience, it is love that is the ultimate proof of the value of the spiritual journey."

Discussion or Journal Questions

1. Do you practice a type of prayer or meditation? How would you describe it?

2. What is your perception of extroverted contemplative prayer?

6
Singing

My life flows on in endless song;
Above earth's lamentation
I hear the sweet, though far-off hymn
That hails a new creation;
Through all the tumult and the strife
I hear the music ringing;
It finds an echo in my soul—
How can I keep from singing?
—Robert Lowry

hen I told one experienced editor of books on spirituality that I was doing research on spiritual practices for extroverts, his immediate response was, "Ah, that would be singing!" And this practice is, indeed, greatly loved by extroverts.

Spontaneous Singing

One expression of that love can be found in Paul Hawker's book *Soul Quest: A Spiritual Odyssey Through 40 Days & 40 Nights of Mountain Solitude.* After I read Paul's book, I emailed him with information about my study. He graciously agreed to participate and to allow me to quote from his book. Paul is an omnivert, and his writing contains many examples of both introverted and extroverted spiritual practices. In this excerpt, he describes one of his favorite practices—raising his voice in song.

On a fine, clear day like the one I was enjoying, New Zealand sunsets are utterly breathtaking. I gazed in awe. What can rival the sun setting into the sea viewed from the top of a mountain on a clear day? It was absolutely majestic, imposing, and wonderful. Thank you, thank you! As I sat there celebrating the Maker's works, and thankful for the dazzling display, I felt as if I was being thanked for enjoying it! The Source was gaining immense pleasure from my pleasure. I hummed and sang any love song that came to mind, trying to express the inexpressible gratitude, amazement, and awe I was feeling. The Platters' *Only You*, Elvis Presley's *Can't Help Falling in Love*, Jimmy Barnes' *(Your Love Keeps Lifting Me) Higher and Higher*, Joe Cocker's *You Are So Beautiful*. Songs seemed the only way to touch what I felt. [1]

Performing

As with every other spiritual practice, singing can be done in an extroverted or introverted way. Bruce Harding, liturgical hymn writer, musician, and omnivert with an introverted inclination, is a good example of one who can move into both spaces in the same performance. He told me that singing and playing his guitar or flute in concerts is a frequent spiritual practice. Sometimes it's an extroverted experience that involves him with the audience—a sense of oneness with them, as well as with God. Sometimes the audience doesn't exist, and Bruce experiences a Flow and enters it.

Linnea Good is an omnivert with an extroverted inclination. She said that many performers who sing and play what is commonly thought of as extroverted music—big-energy, foot-tapping, need-to-get-out-of-your-chair music—are often very introverted people. She herself used to perform from a deep, introverted place, so much so that after concerts she would need to spend some time in her dressing room to summon a more extroverted energy before going out to mingle with the audience. It was sometimes a challenge to shift the energy. So she consciously worked on moving more quickly and easily from one inclination to the other. She told me, "I find it helpful as a composer and performer to be an omnivert. I need to be able to find a balance."

Overcoming Negative Judgments

Many extroverts speak of the joy of group singing, feeling the energy of others as they raise their own voices. "But I can't carry a tune," you might say. You needn't worry. Secular and spiritual choirs and bands often welcome new members and do not rate singing ability as a criterion for inclusion. In fact, I know of a number of choirs that are intended specifically for challenged singers. And the sound they make is incredibly beautiful.

You may feel the urge to sing as a spiritual practice and yet are too shy to do so, even when alone. The cause may very well be that your singing ability was negatively judged earlier in your life. Although anyone can be judged in this way, my hunch is that extroverts get a larger share of it. Why? Because we are so visible. We are more likely to walk around singing than most introverts.

If you have had negative experiences with your singing, I invite you to undertake some healing. Singing is such a great spiritual practice. I was the only girl in third grade who wasn't allowed to be in the school choir. I was told I sung off-key. So during choir I had to remain in an almost empty classroom with three boys who were there because they wouldn't behave. I was mortified! Up until then, I thought I was a great singer and sung every chance I got. But not after that experience.

It was years before I could sing again, and when I did so it was by myself, where no one else could hear me. Over a long period of psychological and spiritual growth, I reached the point where I was willing to sing when others might hear me. But because I still believed I couldn't carry a tune, I tended to sing quietly and lowly, thinking I would be less noticeable that way.

I particularly loved to attend concerts by Linnea Good, whose words you have just read, because she made a point of saying that singing is integral to our life as humans. "It's like breathing," she said. "Some of us are better than others at breathing, but there is no reason why those of us who are not as good should leave it up to the experts." One night after her concert, Linnea approached me and said, "I heard you singing tonight, because you were sitting so close to me." "Oh, dear," I replied. I had shared my singing experience with her some years previously. She smiled at me. "You know what? You were on key. I think it would help you to have a session with a singing teacher. A good voice teacher can help you hear yourself in a new way."

Although I was extremely apprehensive, I did phone a singing teacher. The results of her evaluation were mind-boggling. "You have a pretty voice," she told me. "The problem has been that in trying to be less visible, you've been singing too low for your range. You've been trying to be an alto, when really you're a soprano. Also, its harder to stay on key when you're singing really quietly, as you've been doing. When you sing loudly and within your own range, you are on key." It's taken me a while to change the belief that I am not a good singer.

If you find yourself avoiding spiritual practices that you are really drawn to, such as singing, you diminish yourself by continuing that avoidance. I met an extrovert at a workshop in a city I was visiting. Karen had a speech impediment, which resulted in her talking slowly with a stutter. She had some great insights into our workshop topic, and the other participants were eager for her contribution. She loved to talk. The next day was Sunday, and I attended worship at her church.

Karen read the first Scripture passage. In order to understand what she was saying, I found myself listening more carefully than I usually did. Later I talked with the pastor, who said many people have mentioned that when Karen reads, the congregation moves into a deeper listening mode. The other thing I noticed about Karen's reading was her great joy in speaking God's word. She glowed with happiness. Listening to Karen made this part of worship even more spiritually meaningful than it usually was for me.

Karen had the wisdom to embrace speaking rather than avoid it, even though it was hard for her, and both she and those around her have benefited.

Spiritual Role Models

Louise Rose (1944–)

Music is a perfect metaphor for life itself.

Louise is known internationally as a versatile pianist, vocalist, recording artist, composer, motivational speaker, choral conductor, accompanist, teacher, facilitator, and caring mentor. The Heritage Rose Window in the Alix Goolden Performance Hall of the Victoria Conservatory of Music is dedicated to Louise Rose in recogition of her contribution to music. In 2001 she received an honorary Doctorate of Fine Arts from the University of Victoria.

A quote from her website states that "Louise conducts the two hundred voices of the Victoria Good News Choir. The choir is a community choir in the truest sense of the word. All one needs in order to belong to the choir is the desire to sing. Her philosophy about singing and about much of the rest of life has been passed down to her from her grandmother, who said 'You are worthy simply because you are breathing.' Therefore there are no auditions for the choir."[2]

A former Baptist missionary, Louise believes that the first and last words of every day should be "thank you." Gratitude is her spiritual philosophy. Her most recent recordings are *Cool Yule* and *Lovingly, Louise*.

When I talked with Louise recently, she said that she experiences extroverted energy during concerts: "The choir, the audience, and I do it together—we share the experience. I also plan concerts in an extroverted way. I absolutely must have others share my dream, so I daydream out loud and encourage them to do the same. Writing, however, is where I move into introverted energy. It is a monastic experience for me."

As for singing, I'm learning to make it a part of my spiritual practice. One favorite activity of mine is to play the radio while I'm driving. I change stations frequently, listening for the "right" song. Then I sing it to God. Sometimes, though I'm the one singing, it seems to be a message to me from God. Often the right song is a love song. Sometimes it's a protest song or lament.

So, if you wish, sing in a group or sing alone while going about your daily activities. You may discover, as did spiritual guide and omnivert Augustine of Hippo (354–430), "To sing once is to pray twice."

Discussion or Journal Questions

1. Is singing a spiritual practice for you? If so, how and when would you sing?

2. What are some of your favorite spiritual songs, and what feelings, sensations, or thoughts do they evoke in you?

7
Cultivating Spiritual Friendships

Anyone without a soul friend is like a body without a head.
—Brigit of Kildare (fifth century)

Spiritual friends can help us in many ways. They can give us support and encouragement when spiritual path is rough, and they can help us navigate when we are lost or unable to move past obstacles in our way. A spiritual friend will rejoice with us, grieve with us, listen to us, and love us. Ruth is Jewish and finds her spirituality expressed outwardly in many ways. She writes that her spiritual friend Susan is an extrovert role model for her: "She has a rich life of spirit—she is always working her spiritual muscles!"

Sometimes the most loving thing spiritual friends can do for us is to question us or call us on behavior that is restricting or diminishing us. Thomas Becket, the twelfth-century Archbishop of Canterbury and extrovert, addressed this point when he wrote, "It is dangerous for [those] in power if no one dares to tell them when they go wrong."

I don't know if Brigit of Kildare was an extrovert. (She may have been, since she was abbess of a large and busy monastery in Ireland that included men and women.) Even if she wasn't, however, she spoke to extroverts when she said, in effect, that others who intentionally accompany us on our spiritual path are not just nice to have, they are essential.

Extroverted Soul Friends

A soul friend or spiritual friend of an extrovert is in some ways the same and in other ways different from a soul friend or spiritual friend of an introvert. Many introverts tell me about deep, long-term friendships with others who have made a commitment to be there for them on their spiritual path. They tell me they experience the benefits I listed in the first paragraph of this section. Those benefits appear to be the same for extroverts and introverts. What seems to be different is the dynamics—the forces that produce activity and change in the relationship.

Extroverts often feel a need to share and listen to the insights and experiences of others, while introverts tell me that they rarely feel this need. Another difference is that introverts tend to sort through and process an insight or experience prior to telling their spiritual friend about it, while we extroverts often prefer to do our processing with a friend. Linda, an extrovert, commented about spiritual friendship, "I learn so much about myself by being involved with others. I am a very interactive learner. As I learn, I need to tell people about what I have figured out. I meet a friend once a week, and we talk about our spiritual life and pray together. This is very meaningful for me."

God Will Provide

Max Oliva is an extroverted Jesuit priest living in Canada. His current passion is spirituality and the workplace, and he is close to publishing a book on the topic. When he made a trip far from home to a place he knew would be emotionally taxing, his main concern was whether he would have someone with whom to debrief. He tells the following story in his book *God of Many Loves*:

As part of my Jesuit training, in 1977 I went to Calcutta, India to live for three months. I stayed with the Brothers of the Missionaries of Charity, at their novitiate, and worked with them at Mother Teresa's Home for Dying Destitutes and other places that serve the poor. As I was preparing to leave my home in Berkeley, California for India, I encountered some fear within myself. I had heard stories about the severity of the poverty in Calcutta, that there were thousands of people living on the sidewalks. My anxiety centered on who would be there that I could talk to about what I would be experiencing. As an extrovert, I knew I would either go crazy or give up and come home early if I did not have people to share with. [1]

Max began work at the home for dying destitutes on the day after he arrived in Calcutta.

I was given a pitcher of water, a pan, and a towel and proceeded to the first order of the day—washing the bodies of those in the men's ward. Each man had his own cot. As I slowly made my way from one man to the next, I was aware of how terribly thin each was. My fingers touched bones as I carefully soaped and rinsed these emaciated people. At mid-morning we had a break and were asked to come back in half an hour to help feed the men. I walked over to a spot by the entrance and stood for a few minutes reading a prayer that was hanging from one of the pillars there.

I could see into the men's area from where I stood, could see some of the men I had recently washed. Suddenly, tears started rolling down my cheeks. I knew I could not continue working that day and motioned to one of the other volunteers. He seemed to understand my reaction to the suffering around us and agreed to take me back to the Brothers' House, a bus ride away. Brother Andrew, then General Servant of the Brothers, was visiting at the time and he invited me to have a cup of tea with him. As I sat with him and began giving him an account of the morning, I completely broke down and cried till I had no tears left. He simply sat with me and supported me by his presence. Finally, he suggested I take a few days off, get to know the city a bit, and then let him know if I wanted to return to the Home for Dying Destitutes or go somewhere else.

During those two days, the fear I had felt before leaving home about not having people to talk to about what I was seeing and experiencing resurfaced. I felt comfortable with Brother Andrew, but he was due to leave Calcutta soon. On the second day, I joined the Brothers at Mass. Brother Andrew was the celebrant. The gospel was on the multiplication of the loaves and fish. In his homily, Brother Andrew commented on the fact that after everyone had eaten there was still food left over. "What this means to me," he said, "is that God provides not only what we need but more than we need to do his work." This insight jolted me as I realized it contained the answer to my fears. I had to believe God would provide what I needed—people to share with—and even more than I would need to help me process my feelings and thoughts during my time in Calcutta. And that is precisely what did happen. I met people throughout the summer, in various places, who helped me make sense of what I was going through in order to integrate it. [2]

As this story shows, spiritual friendships do not need to be of long duration. I remember one meaningful conversation I had with an extroverted rabbi as we waited in line to check our bags at the airport. It took forty minutes to reach the check-in desk. As we inched closer, listening to the frustrated grumbles from other passengers, we quietly talked of the difficulty and benefit of learning patience. Talking together was supportive and inspiring for both of us.

Spiritual Guides

Extroverts (and introverts) can also benefit from talking with people trained in spiritual issues. Clergy, pastoral counselors, and spiritual directors will be helpful if they are good listeners and believe extrovert spirituality is valid. Of the extroverts in my study, the majority either were spiritual directors or had had contact with one.

"What is a spiritual director?" you may ask. "I don't want anyone directing my spirituality!" That's good, because a spiritual director does not "direct." The term has been in use for so long that the worldwide organization, Spiritual Directors International, a group of more than 6,000 women and men from a number of faith

Spiritual Role Models

Francis of Assisi (1181 or 1182–1226)

Preach the Gospel at all times, and when necessary use words.

Saint Francis is one of the most beloved spiritual guides of all time. He is popular with people of many faith traditions and with people who do not view themselves as religious.

As a youth, Francis was the life of the party. He led his group of friends on many escapades. He sang, danced, and partied all night.

Then he had a conversion experience and threw his extroverted energy into a relationship with God. He still sang and danced, and spent lots of time with others. Now, however, these activities were under the guidance of his Beloved. Always charismatic and appealing, Francis attracted many to join him. The Franciscan family today has many branches and is made up of both women and men.

I believe Francis was an omnivert. In spite of his extroverted qualities, he felt a strong pull to the more interior life of a monk as well as to the life of a preacher and healer. In order to choose his life path, Francis asked a spiritual brother and sister to pray for divine guidance on his behalf. Both friends subsequently informed Francis that his ministry was to be in the world. Francis immediately set out on a preaching tour. He still, however, spent many hours in his retreat place, a cave, where he could nourish his introvert side.

Francis is known for his call to reform the Christian church, respect and love of nature and animals, mediation skills, simple living, and care of the poor. People still sing his songs, and pray his prayers, particularly his "Canticle of the Creatures." It was Francis who created a new Christian ritual that is now practiced by millions: when the people came for the Christmas Eve service, they saw animals, straw, and a manger.

traditions and spiritualities, decided to keep it. A better way of describing their role is that spiritual directors accompany people on the spiritual path. Effective directors do not tell seekers what to believe or recommend their own religion or type of spirituality. The following description is on the Spiritual Directors International website, www.sdiworld.org:

> Spiritual direction is the process of accompanying people on a spiritual journey. Spiritual direction helps people tell their sacred stories every day. Spiritual direction exists in a context that emphasizes growing closer to God (or the holy or a higher power). Spiritual direction invites a deeper relationship with the spiritual aspect of being human. Spiritual direction is not psychotherapy, counseling, or financial planning.

There are many options for us extroverts who have a desire to speak of our spiritual journey. It is important to monitor the outcome of such contact periodically with another person. A beneficial contact will see our faith deepen in a way that leads to growth in qualities such as love and compassion, and it will help us live more fully into the unique spiritual being each of us is.

Discussion or Journal Questions

1. If you have a spiritual friend, what does the relationship do for you?

2. Do you have any spiritual role models, such as Francis of Assisi, who are arousers of faith for you?

8
Moving Prayer

*"I have a growing conviction that we don't use our bodies
nearly enough in our prayer."*
—Sheila Pritchard

*M*oving prayer can take many forms; dancing, walking, hiking, swaying, using different parts of the body to respond in worship services—the list is limited only by our creativity. For extroverts, who tend to enjoy stimulation, this is a favorite type of spiritual practice.

Movement, of course, always involves our bodies. To make the movement a spiritual practice, however, requires more than stimulation. The stimulation needs to focus us more fully on the divine. Sheila Pritchard, whose quote begins this chapter, describes a number of different types of prayer movement in her book, *The Lost Art of Meditation,* and then cautions that we watch that certain movements do not become routine, no longer holding "a deep meaning for the participants." [1]

One benefit of including our bodies in spiritual practice is that we give ourselves fully to the experience. This encourages a congruence, a harmony between mind, spirit, feelings, and body. We honor the sacredness of our physicality, along with our intellect, emotions, and soul. And when we honor something, we tend to treat it better. In Christianity, as well as some other faith traditions, there have been times when our bodies were seen as sinful and unspiritual, instead of as the temples they truly are. Spiritual director Jennifer Leos says that "physically moving while praying—such as walking" is her favorite spiritual practice.

Walking

Some people find they can keep their attention focused on God more easily when they are walking. Sherry Gaugler wrote, "Currently, I find an 'active' meditation to be what helps me to connect. Some of my strongest meditative times happen when I am walking around a lake near my home. I get into the rhythm of the walk, talk to God about what's going on in my world, and, after I get it all out, find myself connected and open to guidance. And I find I get it. It's a really amazing experience, and something that just formed for me out of the guidance to exercise to care for my body!"

Although I have titled this section "walking," I include here other forms of moving from one place to another. These can include hiking, running, or being transported, such as by a car. A spiritual exercise practiced by some early Celtic Christians involved sitting in a small boat, called a coracle, and letting the wind blow them where it would. They trusted that God would guide them to a place that was right for them, wherever they ended up. The Aboriginal people of Australia commonly experience a divine urge to "walkabout," a spiritual practice in which they walk by themselves for days or weeks. Some people find that not anticipating a particular destination helps them focus their attention on God.

When spiritual walkers keep their awareness directed to God in the outside world, they are involved with an extroverted spiritual practice. Since extroverts are energized by interaction with the outer world, they may experience, as Linda Leone does, that God reaches out to them as energy. She writes, "When I am outside walking, I may feel a warm glow plus a feeling of energy that comes from the earth, up through my feet, like a pulse. I respond to the Spirit's movement in me with love and gratitude."

Pilgrimage

Many extroverts and introverts find that walking to a particular place, usually one seen as sacred, has been a meaningful spiritual practice. A pilgrimage may take many days, weeks, or even months, or it can be as short as a day. Unlike walking in an unstructured manner, the pilgrimage is usually highly structured. Those who have made pilgrimages to famous shrines tell me that the thought that thousands or even millions of other seekers have walked the same path has made the experience more spiritual for them. Preparing for the pilgrimage, walking it, and returning home are all part of the spiritual practice. God is as present when the bags are being unpacked as when the sacred spot is reached.

Do you feel like making a pilgrimage and yet have only a day? In her book *Personal Pilgrimage: One-day Soul Journeys for Busy People,* Viki Hurst gives examples of mini-pilgrimages to specific places close to home. The intention of making the trip a spiritual practice and the attention given to the experience itself are what make it meaningful. Length of time and difficulty do not result in more brownie points with God. It's true that these short pilgrimages are in some ways different from longer pilgrimages. Viki writes, "What all pilgrims seem to have in common, however, is the desire to *move*—both inwardly and outwardly—from where they are, for enlightenment, wholeness, and deepening." [2]

Labyrinth

An increasingly popular spiritual practice that involves movement is the labyrinth. Many Gothic cathedrals have a labyrinth inserted into the floor of the sanctuary. You can find labyrinths in municipal parks, in church parking lots, at retreat centers, and in many other places. I also know of a number of labyrinths that are made of canvas, so they can be taken to different locations.

A labyrinth is not just a Christian spiritual practice; many other faith traditions have a practice that involves walking a structured path to echo the spiritual journey. The labyrinth is not a maze, in which you try to find your way down many incorrect turnings. If you persevere in walking a labyrinth, you will make it to the center and then back out along the same path. The path, however, turns back on itself, and sometimes, as in life, you find yourself farther away from the center than you were a few minutes previously.

As with any spiritual practice, the goal is not to reach a particular point, such as the center. The goal is to move along the path in a focused, prayerful attitude, receptive to the divine. Some walk the labyrinth in an introverted way, keeping their focus inward. Others prayerfully run it, dance it, or interact with others. Extrovert Peter Boles is a frequent labyrinth walker. He writes, "The labyrinth is providing me with the gift of insights from the Divine. As I walk it, I am given images, words, and pictures that speak to my life."

Dance

Dance as prayer may be a structured experience, in which steps are learned, practiced, and done alone or with others; or we may just let the Spirit move us as we sway to music, in private or as part of a group. I have been to a number of dances at church summer camps involving all ages. It's fun to watch people dance in introverted and extroverted ways. The extroverted dancers are very receptive to their environment and interact with those who happen to be nearest, through eye contact or touch. The introverted dancers are respectful of others, yet their energy is turned inward.

Carrie frequently dances her prayer in private. Each prayer dance is different as she uses her body to express joy, sadness, awe, love, praise, contrition, or whatever else she is feeling. The movements that grow out of these emotions form her spiritual practice. I also like to dance, although I usually don't plan it. Sometimes I find myself starting with a sitting prayer and then realize that my body wants to join in more fully.

I have found that my desire to dance is understood and validated as a spiritual practice by some others, and sometimes it's not. Here are two examples. There is a hermitage on the grounds of a cloistered community of nuns where I have spent many wonderful retreats. When my body says, "Dance," I take myself to the chapel and put on some music. Three times, a nun has come into the chapel to clean while I was dancing. Once, the sister smiled at me as she went about her work. Twice, the sisters danced themselves as they continued their activities. They didn't intrude on

Spiritual Role Models

His Holiness the 14th Dalai Lama, Tenzin Gyatso (1934–)

Throughout history people all over the world have identified particular places as sacred, some because of their association with a sacred event, and others due to uplifting qualities intrinsic to the places themselves. . . . I remember being profoundly moved myself when as a young man I first visited the Buddhist holy places in India. It gave me a very special inspiration to think that at this or that place the Buddha himself had meditated and taught. Somehow I felt more closely connected to him and his teaching as a result.

I believe the 14th Dalai Lama is an omnivert. His introvert side is well developed, as he meditates at least five and a half hours a day. He also loves being with people, as he so clearly demonstrates in his autobiography.

A strong theme running through his life story is new friends he has made. Describing a journey, the Dalai Lama writes, "One of the other joys of staying at the Jokhang was the chance to make new friends among the sweepers there. As usual, all my spare time was spent in their company, and I think that they were as sorry when I left as I was."[3]

Since 1959, when the Dalai Lama fled Tibet, his travels encompass the world. "To me," he writes, "one of the most important aspects of my thirty-one years in exile has been my meetings with people from all walks of life."[4]

"Whenever I go abroad, I try to contact as many other religious practitioners as possible, with a view to fostering inter-faith dialogue."[5] As the quotation that began this section demonstrates, he also travels as a spiritual practice.

my space, and I felt very affirmed in my spiritual practice. I still have the image of an older nun, in her habit, dancing from altar to tabernacle with a feather duster in hand!

I also had an unfortunate experience when I made a solitary, directed retreat soon after my mother died. I chose a retreat center I had never been to, some days' travel from home. By the second day of my stay there, I realized that my body was extremely tense and jittery with the pain of my loss. So I took my jittery body to the empty chapel, put on some music, and danced my pain. By the time the music was over, I felt pleasantly drained and very close to God's tender compassion.

After a long nap, I went for my second spiritual direction session. My director began by saying, "I was walking past the chapel when I noticed you dancing and singing. Retreat time is a quiet time, where we slow down and become more receptive to God." I explained about my jittery body, and she responded, "It is common, on the spiritual path, to encounter times of dryness or other difficulty in prayer. We need to persevere, though, and not keep bouncing from practice to practice."

I could see this woman's compassion for me, and I knew that "bouncing" from one type of spiritual practice to another could be a problem. Yet she wasn't hearing my concern. I tried to explain how symptoms of grieving often include poor concentration and tense, fidgety bodies, but she held fast to her advice. I danced in the woods for the remainder of my retreat.

Extreme Movement

When my husband, Bob, read over this section, his first comment was, "What about skydiving? Or rock climbing?" Yes, there are many more extreme methods of movement that folks do, not just for the physical and emotional stimulation but for the spiritual stimulation. One white-water kayaker commented, "I seem to lose my ego when I am focused on staying upright in the water. I feel an incredible rush, along with a sense of oneness with all creation.

And I realize my own fragility as a human being, at the same time as realizing the infiniteness of God. It is very spiritual for me."

Discussion or Journal Questions

1. Do you practice any moving prayer? If so, please describe it and consider the ways in which it helps you.

2. After reading about the varieties of moving prayer, are you interested in trying any? If you are, pick one, try it, and share your experience with a friend.

9
Practicing Spirituality in Groups

We worship because it is natural to respond
to the mystery that irradiates life.
—Marjorie J. Thompson

Spiritual practice in a group is a favorite activity of extroverts when our outgoing spirituality is welcomed. It can be done in a number of ways. Some extroverts favor large worship services, and others gravitate to small prayer or study groups; some attend workshops, retreats, and courses in religious settings, and others prefer secular groups with a spiritual component.

Group Worship

This spiritual practice combines many aspects that appeal to us as extroverts. These aspects include:

- Being part of the energy of other people all focused on the divine
- Sharing spiritual experiences
- Singing and music
- Active involvement
- Movement
- Developing spiritual friendships

When an extrovert finds a welcoming faith community, it can feel like coming home.

Jim Upright is an active member of the United Church of

Canada. He writes, "My church is my extended family. And it's wonderful to worship with family." Sometimes, however, it may take some time of searching to find the right group to worship with. Many extroverts who come to me for counseling tell me of their longing to worship with others.

Often, these folk aren't even sure what their religion is. After we have spent some time exploring their spirituality, their path becomes clearer. I am then able to describe some different types of worshiping communities in my city. When I see their eyes light up, I know the ones they will be checking out. As with any family, each group of worshipers will have their positive and challenging aspects. Some people think they need to wait for the perfect congregation. They're in for a long wait!

The E and I of Worship

Most worship and other spiritual meetings have an ebb and flow to them. There are times for our energy to turn inward, and other times that encourage an outward direction. I know some extroverts who turn off or wait through the "boring" times, since they find the outward mode more enjoyable or stimulating, and some introverts do the same in reverse. A service that includes both modes—extroverted and introverted (E and I)—is a wonderful opportunity to move toward the orientation you tend to avoid. In such a setting, being fully present to the whole service is a way of allowing ourselves to use more of our brains. We stretch ourselves past previous limits and, I hope, begin to experience the value of introversion as well as extroversion. Worship services can be a training ground for holistic spirituality.

Small Spiritual Groups

Some extroverts are part of a small group of people who meet together as a spiritual practice, instead of or in addition to whatever large group they belong to. Prayer meetings, healing groups, Scripture study, book groups, meetings for specific types of people, such

---

Spiritual Role Models

William F. (Billy) Graham (1918–)

It is not the body's posture, but the heart's attitude that counts when we pray.

From a dairy farm in North Carolina, young Billy Graham left to become a Baptist minister. He was ordained in 1939 at age twenty-one. In 1949 he led an evangelical crusade in Los Angeles that brought him wide attention. He is now an internationally known evangelist and chairman of the board of the Billy Graham Evangelistic Association (BGEA).

His biographical profile on the BGEA website states, "Mr. Graham has preached the Gospel to more people in live audiences than anyone else in history—over 210 million people in more than 185 countries and territories—through various meetings, including Mission World and Global Mission. Hundreds of millions more have been reached through television, video, film, and Web casts."

Billy Graham has written twenty-five books, which have sold many millions of copies. He has received numerous awards, including recognition for interfaith tolerance. A number of U.S. presidents and other heads of state have consulted him. He was married to Ruth Graham for sixty-four years and is the father of five children. His autobiography is *Just as I Am.*

---

as parents, businesspeople, or youth—if you search you will find a group that focuses on your particular interests. Barbara Dowding, current president of the Catholic Women's League of Canada (British Columbia and Yukon) stresses that extroverts need small groups with "interactive dialogue."

Secular Groups with a Spiritual Aspect

There are other groups whose focus is not on worship or prayer and yet which are viewed by some of the participants as involving spiritual practice. I'm thinking particularly of the various twelve-step programs. These are attractive to extroverts because personal sharing is encouraged. Since the tradition of Alcoholics Anonymous is to maintain personal anonymity, the following extrovert has chosen not to give her name. This is her story of a twelve-step program being used as a spiritual practice.

I've been sober for seventeen years. Some people walk into an AA meeting and never touch another drop of alcohol. It wasn't like that for me. Once I realized I was out of control and alcohol was ruining my life, I fiddled around for a few years, going to meetings periodically and trying other ways to deal with the urge to drink. No one would have known I was an alcoholic. I went to work and looked fine on the outside. Inside, though, I was empty. I was and still am a practicing Catholic, but during that time I wouldn't let God touch my life. My god was drink.

The Scripture phrase "For where two or three are gathered in my name, I am there," really fits for AA. Members all know we need assistance greater than ourselves to help us with this addiction. Some call this power God, some our Higher Power, others Good Orderly Direction. There are people from all walks of life meeting together, and I can actually feel the divine energy. The meetings are transformative. AA has given me a life rather than an existence.

The spiritual practice of participating in AA meetings has taught me acceptance of others' differences, and I am able to reach out now and sponsor others who are struggling. All of us who make a commitment to AA intentionally work on ourselves in the presence of God. We are taught total surrender to that healing power. AA has taught me to keep my spirituality simple. I frequently use the following words, from the seventh step, as a prayer: "My Creator, I am now willing that you should have all of me, good and bad. I pray that you now remove from me every single defect of character which stands in the way of my usefulness to you and my fellows. Grant me strength, as I go out from here to do your bidding. Amen." [1]

Another way that participating in a secular group can be a spiritual practice is by focusing on the topic in a prayerful way. For example, many artists view their painting or sculpting or song crafting as spiritual. If you are an extrovert artist, you may join a group of artists to be able to talk with others and be energized by their presence. You can, if you choose, bring a faith dimension in to the group for yourself, and the others may or may not know you are viewing your participation as a spiritual practice.

Last January, a number of us church artists—dancers, composers, authors, fine artists, musicians—met for a weeklong retreat. It was the first time we had done this, and it was a wonderful success. The introverts took the space they needed, and we extroverts had lots of listening ears. We all got enough rest, exercise, stimulation, time to work, group worship, and space to share our dreams, difficulties, and joys. We had a week of companionship with others who understand the creative process. We've decided to make this an annual event and have begun a network of church artists for our geographical area, to meet the frequently expressed need of artists to be able to reach out for support, guidance, or just a listening ear.

Discussion or Journal Questions

1. Do you attend any type of group worship? Please describe it.

2. If you do practice group worship, how does it benefit you? Can you think of ways for the benefit to be increased?

10
Spiritual Reading and Writing

Ultimately, what makes reading devotional is a mysterious fusion in the grace of God of the content and our intention to be opened to guidance.
—Patricia Loring

oan Borysenko's writing grew out of "studying the world's spiritual traditions and hearing the personal stories of people's search for God." Reading and writing are frequently used together as a spiritual practice, which is why I've combined them in this chapter. Of course, they can also be done separately.

Reading

Reading becomes a spiritual practice when it is undertaken to explore faith issues that are encountered during the experience. Reading itself can be a kind of introvert spirituality, and we extroverts may use it to become more comfortable with this side of ourselves.

Although in this chapter most of my focus is on reading books, watching movies or television programs can also be used by some extroverts as a spiritual practice. Leslie, who responded to my questionnaire, and her introverted partner, Henri, are members of a spirituality film club. They receive a DVD each month that contains the film as well as questions to consider afterward. Sometimes they watch and discuss the film as a family; sometimes they invite friends. Leslie loves to reflect on the film conversationally and then later engage with Henri about how its messages apply to their individual and family spiritual journeys.

Spiritual Role Models

Joan Borysenko (1945–)

In studying the world's spiritual traditions and hearing the personal stories of people's search for God, it has become clear that the saying "different strokes for different folks" is as true for people's spirituality as it is for their diets and their love lives.

Joan Borysenko's enthusiasm for wholeness and healing has resulted in a blending of science, psychology, and spirituality in a way that has helped many thousands of people throughout the world. A self-identified ambivert (someone who scores midpoint on the extrovert-introvert scale), Joan Borysenko is known for her dynamic, practical, and humorous books and presentations.

She holds a doctorate in medical science from Harvard Medical School and has completed postdoctoral fellowships in experimental pathology, behavioral medicine, and psychoneuroimmunology. She was an instructor in medicine at Harvard until 1988.

Joan Borysenko, who is also a licensed psychologist, was cofounder and former director of the Mind-Body Program at two Harvard Medical School teaching hospitals. Her first book, *Minding the Body, Mending the Mind* (1987), drew on her experience in the Mind-Body Program and became a New York Times bestseller.

She is the author of many other books, including *The Power of the Mind to Heal: Inner Peace for Busy People*, *Saying Yes to Change*, and *Seven Paths to God: The Ways of the Mystic*. She speaks of herself as "interspiritual," working on the common ground of mystical experience where all traditions meet at depth.

Spiritual Role Models

Concepcion Cabrera (1862–1937)

The Lord unrolled before me spiritual panoramas which left me mute in admiration. Suddenly I found myself involved in the most profound secrets of the spiritual life.

Concepcion Cabrera was born in Armida, Mexico. Strongly extroverted and financially comfortable, she enjoyed being a social butterfly. She was married, had nine children, and lived a very full spiritual life.

From the age of nineteen, Concepcion, or "Conchita" as she was often called, had a burning desire for perfection. She had a number of Christian mystical experiences and shared them with her many supporters. She founded two religious orders in Mexico. Conchita described her mystical experiences in a diary that was subsequenty published as *I Am: Eucharistic Meditations on the Gospel*.

One biography states that her children claim they rarely saw her take the time to write, and yet she left 65,000 handwritten pages of mystical meditations.[1] Much of her writing was about the relational aspect of the Trinity. In her diary, Concepcion spoke strongly about the equality of women and men in the spiritual life. She often told others that she had no trouble living a deeply mystical life and a rich life of the world.

Reading as an introverted practice would only involve the reader. To make the practice more extroverted, some people read aloud in a group and discuss issues and points as they are mentioned in the reading. Others read alone and then meet in book or study groups to process and discuss their experience.

One spiritual practice that starts with reading is to peruse a

Scriptural parable or other short spiritual story and then sit quietly in meditation, open to any meaning or guidance that unfolds. Alternatively, some people follow the reading by imagining themselves in the scene they have just read. If you do this, try to bring the scene alive as vividly as possible by employing all your senses in your imagination. You may find yourself in the scene as yourself or as one or more of the characters. After the scene ends, you may meditate on the experience, talk with others, or write about it.

Another type of spiritual practice involves more deliberate reading of a Scripture passage or the writings of someone we respect as a spiritual guide. Reading slowly and aloud may enable us to be touched on a deeper level by the meanings of the text. Repetitive reading deepens the experience and further slows us down. Remember, we extroverts have a tendency to be impulsive. It may take us a number of repetitions before we move past our initial, impulsive understanding of the text, to a meaning that speaks more fully to our lives.

Writing

As we read and reread the text, usually a word or phrase will repeatedly snag our attention. We then may stop reading and meditate on that word or phrase. Or we may write. Spiritual writing often grows out of spiritual reading. It can take many forms, including structured or unstructured journaling, letters, essays, sermons, poems, or songs. Here is an example of spiritual writing as one of several spiritual practices:

Margaret Lewis is a mentor, meditation facilitator, and spiritual director from California. She wrote, "I tend to experience God very directly, largely through writing and contemplative prayers. I had an experience of feeling led to the oceanside, where I sat for several hours. Nothing happened. Frustrated that I had come in vain, I marched myself up the cliff to return to my car, when I heard the words to a favorite hymn, 'You Are Being Called to Come Forth.' I turned, wept, sat down right where I was, and proceeded to write a short essay that spoke to me very clearly. In fact,

I carried that essay with me for several years as a reminder of the guidance I had been given."

We may find that writing becomes an introverted activity for us, and no one but God ever sees or hears what we have put down on paper. Barbara Gibson, an extroverted spiritual director in Washington State, finds writing "morning pages" and poetry particularly helpful spiritual practices.

Alternatively, we may write as an extroverted experience. Some seekers combine to cowrite a book or song, or team up to create a workshop or retreat. Doing an activity together as a spiritual practice forms or deepens spiritual friendships. I have attended workshops where as a group we were given a spiritual writing activity. Each member contributed a belief or insight on a particular topic, which was then written as a poem. The extroverts happily jumped into this activity. The introverts were more tentative. We realized that the resulting poem could never have been written by any one of us.

A type of spiritual writing I call extroverted is one in which we converse with the divine. We may find that an entry in our journal almost writes itself, or when we pose a written question or concern we may find that we "hear" a response. Almost every poem I've written has woken me out of sleep in the early morning hours. At such times I sense God's presence and an invitation to cocreate. So, on goes the computer, and the poem is born.

For my book "I'd Say Yes God, If I Knew What You Wanted," Stephen Berer told me how, through poetry, he was "wooed" back to being a Jew. "I was denying my spirituality; I was denying G-d; I was denying being a Jew. Then the poetry started. I would experience a compelling image or a line from a text. It stayed with me, inviting me to move into it, to develop a relationship with it, to keep working it until I had written it correctly. Once I opened to the image, information came out in a stream that was too powerful to dam." [2] Stephen told me that, in hindsight, he realized the divine had invited him into a process of spiritual discernment. As he worked with the image or text and decided what to write, he was unconsciously partnering with God. The resulting poem, he knew, was beyond his powers to create alone. Stephen said each poem had "a certain elegance, a lucidity, complexity, and simplicity."

Spiritual writing can bear a variety of fruits. It may help us clarify, process, or explore thoughts, feelings, and experiences. You may find it a good activity for praising, demonstrating love, expressing gratitude, or partnering with God in order to help others. I have repeatedly discovered that when I feel a strong divine urge to write a book or article, although I write with the intent to help others, the process of writing provides me with the healing and growth I need at that time in my life.

You can write anywhere there is something to write with and write on. Although many writers gravitate to quiet spaces, some extroverts find that composing goes easier in the midst of others. As Cathie Caimano wrote, "I really like silence, but I am much more comfortable when there are others around. I often write sermons in crowded coffee shops, for example."

Discussion or Journal Questions

1. Do you practice spiritual reading? If so, please describe your practice and how it helps you.

2. Do you practice spiritual writing? If so, please describe your practice and how it helps you.

11
Praying in Nature

If prayer is considered only an indoor activity
we shall miss out on the opportunity to worship
in the most beautiful temple ever created: the cosmos.
—Edward M. Hays

The quotation above was taken from Ed Hays's book *Pray All Ways*. It contains chapters with titles such as "Play as Prayer" and "How to Pray with Your Feet." Although the book is not specifically on the topic of extroversion, one study participant wrote that she found it particularly helpful in affirming her spiritual practices and giving suggestions to expand her repertoire.

The twelfth-century mystic Hildegard of Bingen spoke of the Holy Spirit as the "greening power of God." Many extroverts and introverts say that being in nature opens them to the Holy. Joyce Rupp, who gave me the idea of writing this book, has coauthored one with Macrina Wiederkehr titled *The Circle of Life: The Heart's Journey Through the Seasons*. It is beautifully illustrated by Mary Southard. The authors write, "The four seasons have much to teach us. When we connect our story to Earth's story we gain insight, strength, and courage to live our own evolving and growth-filled journey around the sun. If we listen closely and carefully to the wisdom of each season we will move beautifully and confidently within our magnificent circle of life." [1]

Some spiritual practices are described below that may help you interact with the rest of creation. As you consider these practices, think about the words of Emily Dickinson:

Some keep the Sabbath going to Church—
I keep it staying at Home—
With a Bobolink for a Chorister—
and an Orchard, for a Dome. [2]

Gardening

Dirty fingernails, aching knees, endless weed-pulling—how can this be a spiritual practice? Well, those who know, know. A gardening friend tells me that, for her, even perusing seed catalogues in the depths of winter elicits a feeling of closeness to her Creator: "I know we're in partnership. I buy and plant the seeds. My Partner provides the soil and rain. This is *our* garden."

There are many books about gardening as a spiritual practice. In *The Sacred Garden*, Patricia Barrett gives many examples of the sacredness of creation and says that even interacting with potted plants can open us to the divine. She believes that any time we open to the beauty of the natural world, we naturally move into prayer.[3]

Gardening is often done in an introverted manner, and yet a few friends working together can turn the activity into an extroverted spiritual practice. For those who live in apartments, community garden plots are very popular. In such circumstances, some people specifically choose their gardening time to coincide with that of others, so their gardening becomes a time for sharing.

Caring for the Environment

With our desire to be actively involved with others, many extroverts join groups to care for Mother Earth. Some speak of their service as spiritual practice. They interpret actively the divine call to be good stewards of the earth, pointing out that after we were created in the divine likeness, God blessed us and said to us, "Be fruitful and multiply, and fill the earth and subdue it; and have dominion over the fish of the sea and over the birds of the air and over every living thing that moves upon the earth" (Genesis 1:28).

Richard Rohr is an extroverted Franciscan priest, author of many books, and director of the Center for Action and Contemplation in Albuquerque. He cautions people who become passionate about active service to find a balance by including some contemplative spiritual practice. It is a challenge for us extroverts who become passionate about our interests to take time to slow down and turn inward.

Types of service in nature can vary widely, including fighting forest fires; transforming a needle-littered, garbage-strewn inner-city lot into a green space safe for children; helping the ecological balance by providing more marshland for waterfowl; and educating the public to be more sensitive to the environment. Of course, many people do activities such as these without thinking of them as a spiritual practice. Yet when I spoke recently to a volunteer in a desert information center, the young woman became very animated as she told me how grounded and in harmony with all creation she feels when she stands in the desert night with stars blazing above her: "You just have to know there's a Creator who loves us. So I say 'thank you' and 'I love you' by volunteering here at the center."

Movement in Nature

When I think of the spiritual practice of walking or hiking in nature, Henry David Thoreau comes immediately to mind. His whole spiritual life was focused on the natural world. In his 1851 essay for *Atlantic Monthly* titled "Walking," Thoreau wrote, "When I would re-create myself, I seek the darkest wood, the thickest and most interminable, and to the citizen, most dismal, swamp. I enter a swamp as a sacred place, a *sanctum sanctorum*. There is the strength—the marrow of Nature."

Movement in nature may be a slow meander or a vigorous hike. Su-Lee, a young immigrant from Hong Kong, wrote, "Swimming is a particularly powerful spiritual grounding practice for me. I'll do it in a pool if I have no other option, but outside is best." Movement in nature may open us to introvert energy if done alone, or we may find the spiritual aspect heightened by being part of a group of friends or a member of a hiking or canoe club.

Retreats, Workshops, and Holidays in Nature

Some people specifically choose retreat centers or holidays based on the natural surroundings. Being in a particular location can enhance the sacred feeling of an experience. Retreat Centers International has an extensive list of places in North America where seekers can find the form of nature that appeals most to them. Other countries have similar organizations. I like to choose a holiday or retreat in a natural environment that is foreign to me. This makes me feel more vulnerable and aware of my surroundings, which heightens my sensitivity and receptivity to God.

Nature Pilgrimage

We have already spoken of traveling as a pilgrim to some sacred place. For a number of seekers, this works best if the sacred place is not associated with people. Daniel wrote, "When I'm feeling ungrounded or stressed in my life, I set aside a day or longer and make a pilgrimage to flowing water. It reminds me of my mother's womb, of the waters of my baptism, of the fact that our bodies are mostly composed of water. There is a particular spot I go a few times a year which is a day's drive from home. This is my own pilgrimage destination."

Traditional spiritual practices of many aboriginal peoples include nature pilgrimages or "vision quests." The spiritual guide Black Elk writes, "Then I was standing on the highest mountain of them all, and round about beneath me was the whole hoop of the world. And while I stood there I saw more than I can tell and I understood more than I saw; for I was seeing in a sacred manner the shapes of all things in the spirit, and the shape of all shapes as they must live together like one being. And I saw that the sacred hoop of my people was one of many hoops that made one circle, wide as daylight and as starlight, and in the center grew one mighty flowering tree to shelter all the children of one mother and one father. And I saw that it was holy." [4]

Spiritual Photography

My introvert husband, Bob, told me, "Photography as a creative and spiritual practice is for me an invitation to discover wonder and delight in the created world. I mostly take photos of flowers and trees. And as I walk through the neighborhood or sometimes to far-off places, I am intensely focused on all that lies around me. When I find a design that delights me, I move into harmony with it. Then the challenge is in composing and presenting the image that delights, in a balanced, dramatic way within a two-dimensional framed format."

Do you feel an interest in the spiritual practice of photography, yet wish it to be more extroverted? Grab a few friends and cameras, or attend one of the many spiritual photography retreats and workshops around the world. For example, in April 2007 the sixth annual Kanuga Photography Retreat was held in North Carolina. There, students ranged from beginners to professionals and took courses such as Contemplative Portraits, Seeing with a Digital Camera, Seeing and Photographing Landscapes of the Spirit, and Soul Sharing. [5]

Caring for Animals

Mary Lou Randour is the author of *Animal Grace: Entering a Spiritual Relationship with Our Fellow Creatures*. "Quite simply," she writes, "animals teach us about love: how to love, how to enjoy being loved, how loving itself is an activity that generates more love, radiating out and encompassing an ever larger circle of others. Animals propel us into an 'economy of abundance.' They teach us the language of the spirit. Through our contact with animals we can learn to overcome the limits imposed by difference; we can reach beyond the walls we have erected between the mundane and the sacred." [6]

Spiritual Role Models

Nahman of Bratslav (1772–1811)

David danced before the LORD *with all his might; David was girded with a linen ephod. So David and all the house of Israel brought up the ark of the* LORD *with shouting, and with the sound of the trumpet.*

As the ark of the Lord came into the city of David, Michal daughter of Daul looked out of the window, and saw King David leaping and dancing before the LORD. *(2 Samuel 6:14-16)*

King David set a precedent that Rabbi Nahman of Bratslav enthusiastically followed. Rabbi Nahman was a Hasidic master, preacher, and religious thinker. He was a great-grandson of the Baal Shem Tov, the founder of Hasidism. Among other spiritual practices he was known for, Rabbi Nahman frequently danced in a joyfully abandoned manner. Two Jewish women in my study mentioned that they viewed Rabbi Nahman as a model of extroverted spirituality. Charlotte Sutker said, "He advocated spending an hour a day outside shouting to God at the top of your lungs—calling out all your pain—and to hug trees. Perhaps he was the first tree hugger."

Rabbi Nahman viewed nature as sacred. In his preaching, "Nahman depicts the task of the religious person as that of seeking out the particular and unique bits of holiness in each aspect of creation, in each tree or blade of grass, in each person. Such a one becomes a channel for these individualized sparks to return to God" or "a weaver, drawing the various strands of holiness together into a proper whole." [7]

There have been times in my life when, in grief or pain, I closed myself off from people and God. My cat, and later my two dogs, wouldn't let me get away with this. Their loving and insistent demands for attention and connection kept me from continuing this unhealthy path. Many people find that in caring for an animal—whether helping at a wildlife rehabilitation center, putting out a feeder for the birds, or making a commitment to a lifetime relationship with a companion animal—they receive much more psychological and spiritual benefit than they ever could have imagined.

Nature: God's Invitation

In my work in children's spirituality I have interviewed many people who said their very first experience of the sacred was in nature. These people reported that the experience occurred while walking in a field or observing an animal, even though at the time they may not have been seeking God out. They felt the sacred come close at that time. They experienced a sense of wonder, oneness, awe, and immense love. They may even have "heard" guiding words as they sat by the seashore or gazed into the limpid eyes of a deer.

Spiritual director and psychotherapist Charlotte Sutker of Victoria, British Columbia, wrote about growing up in a secular Jewish family: "Mostly I knew God through nature, as we were a very sporty, outdoorsy family. And my first husband was also outdoorsy. I felt God even more strongly when he and I spent time in the wilderness." Charlotte also told me about Nahman of Bratslav, who wrote of the sacredness of nature, and whom she considered an extroverted spiritual role model.

Discussion or Journal Questions

1. Have you had a spiritual experience while out in nature? If so, please describe it and tell what it meant to you.

2. What does the following Scripture passage mean to you? "Be fruitful and multiply, and fill the earth and subdue it; and have dominion over the fish of the sea and over the birds of the air and over every living thing that moves upon the earth" (Genesis 1:28).

Part Three

Living More Deeply into Spiritual Extroversion

12
Challenges of Being Extroverted Persons of Faith

How many apparent obstacles in life are really openings through which new invitations come?
—Gerald May

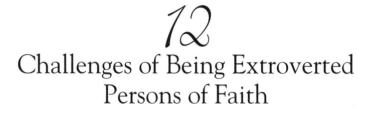 eing an extrovert has benefits and provides opportunities, as we have seen. However, it can also lead to challenges that must be dealt with in order for us to heal and grow. In this chapter, we'll look at some of the special challenges encountered by extroverts of faith. Each of the following challenges focuses on a characteristic common in extroverts. The characteristics are on a continuum: at one end, the characteristic causes us to stumble frequently on our spiritual path; at the other end, the characteristic supports and nurtures us on our journey through life.

As you deal with your challenges, the point is not to eliminate the characteristics but to transform them into useful habits and practices. You can do this by first making yourself aware of the characteristic, as well as where it is on your personal continuum. As I describe each challenge, I invite you to reflect on how it plays out in your own life: What attitudes, beliefs, and behaviors keep you stuck in a negative pattern? As you become more self-aware, you can begin to work on the characteristic, practicing new attitudes, beliefs, and behaviors. You will find yourself slowly moving up the continuum and will begin to find that the same characteristic that once diminished you now enhances you. What started as a challenge will begin contributing to your spiritual and psychological growth, and you will become a freer, more loving person.

Challenge 1. Are You Impulsive or Spontaneous?

The continuum here is from impulsivity (acting without really thinking) to spontaneity (being gracefully natural and unrestrained).

When I facilitate workshops, I usually have participants form small groups for a variety of activities. Invariably, some of the extroverts are enthusiastic and eager to share, almost squirming in their seats as they wait for the group to begin its task. Often, they don't wait until everyone is ready to listen, instead blurting out their contribution as soon as a few people are seated.

There are two problems with this. First, since the introverts may still be processing the instructions, the extroverts' contributions won't be heard by many in the group. It is unlikely that anyone will respond, so the extroverts may think others don't value their sharing.

The second problem involves the importance the extroverts attach to their contributions. If extroverts speak impulsively, they blurt out the first thing on their minds. Then, after a few others have shared, the extroverts often realize they have more important things to say. And there may not be another opportunity!

To deal with this issue, when I send workshop participants off to form small groups I usually say something like this: "I suggest that when you form your groups, you first choose someone to be facilitator. That person can watch the time and make sure everyone who wishes to speak gets a chance. Then I suggest that the group be silent for fifteen seconds. This silence will allow the extroverts to get past the first 'blurt' so that they will have a better chance of sharing what is most important to them about the topic. It also allows time for introverts to process the instructions and be ready to share. Otherwise, the extroverts may grab the conversational ball and keep it." Usually the participants laugh at my words. Later, though, I frequently receive thanks from both extroverts and introverts for beginning the activity in this way.

Spiritual Role Models

William Sloane Coffin Jr. (1924–2006)

So don't let money tell you who you are. Don't let power tell you who you are. Don't let enemies and—for God's sake—don't let your sins tell you who you are. Don't prove yourself. That's taken care of. All we have to do is express ourselves.

William Sloane Coffin, a Presbyterian minister, was known as a social activist and a civil rights and antiwar campaigner. He supported interfaith dialogue and was a strong proponent of nuclear disarmament.

Coffin was arrested as one of Martin Luther King, Jr.'s freedom riders in the early 1960s. As chaplain of Yale University, he was a vocal opponent of the Vietnam War. His speaking against the war turned into civil disobedience. He was charged with conspiracy to encourage draft evasion and was tried along with a group of other protesters such as Benjamin Spock. The group members were convicted but won on appeal.

During the last years of his life, Coffin focused on antiwar and antinuclear campaigns. He did not speak of himself as a pacifist, however. Coffin recommended that an international force intervene for crimes such as genocide. He was very verbal in his criticism of the Persian Gulf War and the 2003 invasion of Iraq. Up until his death, William Sloane Coffin was a charismatic, deeply spiritual extrovert.

Learning to Be Spontaneous

We extroverts are always processing data. We also have a strong urge to share, to contribute, to act. So when we find ourselves with a chance to speak, we may quickly say what's on our mind at that moment. This is impulsivity. The sharing may not be what we would say if we took even a few moments to consider our contribution. We may also act without thinking through the implications of our behaviors. Impulsivity keeps us in shallow waters of thought and action.

Spontaneity, the other end of this continuum, is indeed "gracefully natural and unrestrained." People who are spontaneous are able to embrace the moment flexibly. They can sense and respond to that moment, to meet their own or another's unexpected needs. People who act spontaneously see the reality of a situation and deal with it swiftly and decisively, while being grounded in "divine flow."

Spontaneous people know that some things need to be planned, and the planning enhances their spontaneity. Kathleen Finley is a writer and spiritual guide who explores issues of practical spirituality, including ways to pray with all one's senses, and issues of spirituality as it relates to the realities of marriage and family life. Her books include *Savoring God: Praying with All Our Senses; The Liturgy of Motherhood: Moments of Grace;* and *Prayers for the Newly Married.* She writes, "To put it informally, prayer is time to 'hang out' with God. But often, good quality 'hanging out'—whether with a friend or with God—may take a bit of planning and clearing the schedule to help it happen." [1]

What Keeps Us in Impulsivity

I have a history of being a very impulsive person. Sometimes I still am. I resisted changing for some time, because I thought losing my impulsivity would diminish me. In talking to other extroverts, I discovered that we shared some beliefs and characteristics that kept us stuck in impulsive patterns. Do any of these sound familiar?

- I'm an intuitive person, so I need to say the first thing that comes to me or I'll lose it.
- I like the rush I get from rapid-fire repartee.
- It's hard work to think about each thing I say.
- I want to be sure I get my two cents' worth in.
- It's boring to slow my responses down.

I have come to the awareness that when I am at my most impulsive, I am very self-centered. I'm always planning my next response and wondering what others think of my contributions. Later, I tend to evaluate the conversation in terms of winning or losing. Did I win? Did I impress people or convince them that my comments were better than theirs? In contrast, when I am spontaneous I value others as well as myself. My attention is very much in the present, and I want all parties in the conversation to win.

It does take work to change from impulsivity to spontaneity. To do it, at first I consciously held back in conversations, when previously I had been one of the first to speak. Then I thought about my goal in speaking and shifted from a desire to enhance myself to a desire to enhance the conversation or relationship. In the beginning I felt frustrated. It was hard to keep from blurting out my thoughts. Over time, though, I am experiencing and thoroughly enjoying "gracefully natural and unrestrained spontaneity."

Challenge 2. Are You Known for Unfocused Chatter or Focused Talk?

Have you ever been called a chatterbox? Do you tend to jump from topic to topic, bring in a great amount of detail, or frequently speak about the past in order to explain what you are saying in the present? This is quite a common conversational pattern for extroverts. And it drives introverts crazy! Of course, that is not reason enough to change. But there are other reasons.

I know that when I have felt off-center, ungrounded, too vulnerable, or worried that I am being judged, I am more likely to

Spiritual Role Models

Simon Peter (first century)

"Even though all become deserters, I will not." —Mark 14:29

Jesus met the fisherman Simon Peter in Capernaum. Peter's household included his wife and mother-in-law. (Paul, in 1 Corinthians, states that Peter's wife was a believer and accompanied her husband on his preaching missions.) After Jesus' death, Peter was considered the head of the newly formed church.

Accounts of Peter do not call him an extrovert. It is highly unlikely, though, that someone so impulsive could be an introvert! Here is one of the many situations where Peter spoke or acted before he thought: During the Last Supper, Jesus took a towel and basin and began to wash his followers' feet. "He came to Simon Peter, who said to him, 'Lord, are you going to wash my feet?' Jesus answered, 'You do not know now what I am doing, but later you will understand.' Peter said to him, 'You will never wash my feet.' Jesus answered, 'Unless I wash you, you have no share with me.' Simon Peter said to him, 'Lord, not my feet only but also my hands and my head!'" (John 13:6-9).

Simon impulsively protested the impropriety of the master's washing his followers' feet and didn't listen to Jesus' response. When Jesus explained further, Peter immediately went from one extreme to the other and requested that Jesus wash more than his feet.

Bart D. Ehrman says that Peter's appeal is his very real humanness. "He is someone whom followers of Jesus have been able to relate to: good-hearted and eager to please but, when it comes to the moment, vacillating, impetuous, unreliable."[2]

engage in unfocused chatter. It gives me the illusion that I am in charge of the situation. In reality, the chatter alienates others and does not allow me to engage with my true feelings or meet my current needs.

Unfocused chatter is not helpful for either party in the conversation. When we extroverts give in to it, we are reacting rather than responding. In psychology, *reacting* to a situation means acting blindly, taking no responsibility for ourselves or our actions. It is also very impulsive. Some people react in negative ways, which is called *triggering*. The triggered reaction is usually seen as excessive by others. For example, if I have had a bad experience with an authority figure in the far past, I might trigger on any statement I currently perceive as controlling. If you say, "I'm not so keen on that idea of yours," I may trigger and hotly protest, "You always want your own way! I'm not your slave."

In contrast, *responding* to a situation means acting with awareness, taking responsibility for myself and my actions. It means being aware of woundedness that may heighten my tendency to trigger. Responding also implies I am sensitive to the other person and to the context of our conversation, including limitations such as time constraints and confidentiality issues.

If unfocused chatter is at one end of the continuum, focused talk is at the other. Focused talk has a concentrated and unified quality to it. When we engage in it, we have a sense of where we want to go in a conversation, and we let go of impulses that try to pull us away from our goal.

Encouraging Focused Talk

Over the years, I have learned two strategies to help change unfocused chatter to focused talk. The first is frequently to do a quick internal status check. If I am aware of anything negative, such as feeling judged, that awareness tends to free me up to have a choice of responses.

The second strategy is to develop an internal tracking mechanism that lets me know if I am speaking a lot. "A lot" is not necessarily bad, since it's important to share, but I don't want to dominate a conversation or communicate so much material that my introvert listener is overwhelmed. So if my internal tracking guide says, "You're starting on the second example of that concept" or "You're now moving to the past" or "You've been talking for five minutes straight," I can evaluate the situation and choose whether or not to stop talking.

Focused Talk for E's and I's

Introverts are experts at focused talk. Their way of doing it, though, is different from the way extroverts do it. We extroverts enjoy sorting through and processing information out loud, with others. This pattern, besides being enjoyable, is helpful to us. Introverts, on the other hand, tend to sort through and process on their own. They may not wish to talk about something they haven't had time to think about previously.

Also, when extroverts explore spiritual experiences and issues, we often bring in examples from other people or from the past. This is not necessarily being scattered or tangential. Sometimes speaking of other examples helps us focus on our own experience. We also love to illustrate our stories with a lot of detail. But we don't expect introverts, or even other extroverts, to remember it all. In the next chapter I will give introverts suggestions to help them keep from becoming overwhelmed by extroverts' wide-ranging and yet focused talk.

Challenge 3. Are You a Stimulation Junkie or Living a Multifaceted Spirituality?

In *The Introvert Advantage: How to Survive in an Extrovert World*, author Marti Olsen Laney describes a number of studies of extroverts' brains that show that the amount of stimulation and novelty we need, enjoy, and can handle would overwhelm and "turn off" an introvert. [3] Yet if we are always seeking stimulation, we become slaves to our extroversion.

If our need for stimulation is unchecked, we will find ourselves grabbing every new spiritual practice or concept that comes our way. We won't spend enough time with any one practice to get to know its benefits before we discover a new practice and drop the old one. It's a little bit like divorcing after the honeymoon so that we can quickly remarry and have another honeymoon! Being a stimulation junkie keeps us swimming in the shallows of the spiritual life. Bill Petro, a faculty member of the West Virginia Institute for Spirituality, is an introvert who is sensitive to the spiritual needs of extroverts. He wrote, "I find that there is often a restlessness and searching in extroverts for the next thing to do. I also see that they are sometimes tempted to excessive good."

The healthy end of this continuum is living a multifaceted spirituality. Many of us extroverts feel a benefit in having a number of different spiritual practices in our lives at any one time. Our introvert friends likely roll their eyes when we talk about our many spiritual practices.

Just because a spiritual practice is enjoyable or beneficial, though, is not enough reason to include it as a frequent practice; more is not necessarily better. We need to evaluate how adding the practice will affect our other practices, our time, energy level, and other factors. We need to find a creative balance in our spiritual life. Oralee Stiles works at the Interfaith Spiritual Center in Portland, Oregon. She wrote, "My practices change, often every few months, although as I wrote this I realize I have some that have lasted for many years."

How do we determine which spiritual practices are best for us at any one time? That definitely is a question for spiritual discernment. I believe that God will invite us to the practices that are most nurturing at any given point in our lives. Here is an example, from my own experience:

In 2001, I was on a cross-Canada workshop and lecture tour for my book *I'd Say Yes, God, If I Knew What You Wanted*. Many times a week I was teaching people to listen more effectively to divine guidance. But I wasn't listening well myself! I was spending a lot of time sitting in cars and planes. My body really needed more exercise, but when I got a break I made excuses to sit or lie down.

I was getting divine nudges in dreams and in prayer that encouraged me to move my body, but I ignored them. Halfway through the tour I had booked myself into a retreat center for a three-day break. When I arrived at the center and met with Kevin, the man who was to be my spiritual director, I told him I was really looking forward to some quiet time with God. Even though I was an extrovert, I was "peopled out"—too much excitement and stimulation. I wanted peace. I was thinking longingly of some extended periods of sitting prayer.

Kevin listened and then asked me to assess how I was doing in all the dimensions of my life at that moment: emotional, mental, spiritual, and physical. I left the physical to the last. When I said I had been sitting for long drives and plane rides, Kevin asked if I was treating my body with the love and care it deserved. I started to squirm and then remembered the dream and prayer nudges. Together we explored my call from God to treat my body with respect. We spoke of ways to have the quiet time alone with God that I craved—in movement, not in long sessions of sitting. That was the type of spiritual practice I most needed, and I left the retreat center refreshed.

Challenge 4. Are You Lost in Space or Befriending Silence?

Do you get panicky when there is a lull in the conversation? Do you tend to jump in to fill the empty space? And does the thought of a retreat where the participants remain silent for five days send your anxiety soaring? Many extroverts are not comfortable with silence. In fact, we can feel lost when there are too many conversational spaces.

Silence is a friend to introverts. They snuggle into it in order to process information, feelings, and thoughts. They use it to catch their mental breath and decide how they want the conversation to progress. They enjoy companionable silences when both members of the conversation sit quietly in love or gratitude.

Would you like to have those experiences that introverts have? If so, you need to befriend silence. You may already have made a start, because many extroverts feel the urge for more balance in this area. There is benefit in cultivating silence in spiritual practice. Interior quietness encourages listening to God. We are more likely to hear the guidance and support that we need. We are also more likely to be drawn to the deeper experiences of contemplation, including a merging with the divine, called unitive prayer.

Sherry Gaugler shared with me her realization that silence was friendly:

> The first silent retreat I ever attended changed my life. I went to the retreat with an introverted friend, who knew the silence was coming and was a little afraid for me, as I have always been a bit of a chatty girl. At first, I didn't know what to do with myself. It was a weekend retreat, and the silence started on Friday night, so many went to bed. I didn't want to go to bed, so I grabbed a book and blanket and hung out in the common area of the facility until I was sleepy.
>
> The next day I noticed my head racing. Thoughts were running through nonstop, not all of them pleasant. I had no choice but to let them run. After a while I realized an interesting thing: I was finding out what it was like to have a thought complete itself without interruption from outside factors or, frankly, from me as I created distractions. I'm not sure I had ever experienced that before. I was also taking time to notice things around me—people, nature, sounds, scents—and even in silence I still felt connected to the world.
>
> When we broke the silence, it was very difficult for me. I actually had to leave the facility for a while to gradually enter back into the world of sound.
>
> I am so grateful for that experience. I never would have taken time for silence, but because of the retreat I felt I had been given permission to have it in my life. Silence is now a part of how I live, and I have learned to gain connection there, as well as through being with others.

Sherry jumped into a silent retreat before she had done much work on the practice of silence, and she received many benefits.

Spiritual Guides

Kathi Bentall

Kathi Bentall is a spiritual director and retreat leader in Vancouver, B.C., Canada. She is a community member of the Rivendell Retreat Centre on Bowen Island and is a volunteer at The Listening Post in Vancouver's Downtown Eastside.

"I have been aware of the place of silence at different times and in various ways throughout the spiritual journey. When I am supporting others, I am not willing to impose it, yet at the same time I hold a deep belief of the value of entering into silence for both extroverts and introverts. Reflecting on the place of extroversion as a valid preference; [it] calls me to be mindful of any judgment that may slip in. Maybe the reminder is to be aware of different ways of being in the silence—as the comments on extroverted and introverted contemplative prayer indicate."

Most of us, though, will want to build up more slowly. One good way to start is by taking moments during the day, and particularly during conversations, to let your thoughts rest. It will be easier to release your thoughts if you use all your senses to be in your present reality. Practice being present without internal judgment or commentary.

Extrovert Renee Koenig of Melbourne Beach, Florida, found that befriending silence has made her a more effective helper of both extroverts and introverts. She finds she can now listen more deeply. "I am more appropriate. I can let silence reign even in a social situation. I used to be ready to fill silence with another topic so there was no lapse in conversation. Now it is no longer an effort for me to allow, even invite, that kind of silence. I think this represents growth and more balance."

Activity

We've discussed four challenges that extroverts frequently experience. The healthy end of the continuum on three of them—spontaneity, focused talk, and multifaceted spirituality—encourages us to live our extroversion differently. The last, befriending silence, asks us to adopt an introverted practice. The following activity explores these challenges in your own life.

Characteristic Continuum

The four lines below represent the continuums for the four challenges we have discussed. Make a mark on each line corresponding to where you are now in the continuum. Then answer the following questions.

_____

impulsive   spontaneous

_____

unfocused chatter   focused talk

_____

stimulation junkie   multifaceted spirituality

_____

lost in space   befriending silence

1. What is it like for you to be where are you now?
2. What beliefs, attitudes, or behaviors keep you there?
3. If you wish to move on the continuum to transform this characteristic, what do you need to do?

Discussion or Journal Questions

1. Choose one challenge described above and describe how it plays out in your life. Do you wish it to move on the continuum? What might be one way to do that?

2. Do you know of an extrovert who is spontaneous, befriends silence, engages in focused talk, and has a multifaceted spirituality? What is it like to be in contact with that person?

13
Tips for Those Who Love
Extroverts

*Let us then pursue what makes for peace
and for mutual upbuilding.*
—Paul of Tarsus

*T*he goal of this chapter is to share some tips for you introverts who wish to support extroverts on their spiritual path. You may be a parent, partner, friend, pastor, counselor, or spiritual director. You may interact with extroverts, in a helping capacity, rarely or every day of your lives. Whatever the case, it is important that your relationships with extroverts be "win-win." Extroverts can benefit from this chapter by gaining a deeper understanding of the difficulty some introverts have with our outgoing nature.

Unless introverts find some way to honor the characteristics and preferences of the extrovert, they may, out of self-defense, try to "introvertize" the extrovert. I started this book with an example of how I became aware that my extroverted energy was negatively affecting a relationship. The realization came to me that I was like Tigger, the bouncy tiger in A. A. Milne's "Winnie the Pooh" stories. Here is one of the stories, which clearly demonstrates how judging extroverts restricts the judger as well.

In Milne's book *The House at Pooh Corner*, the extroverted Tigger is a delight to a number of the inhabitants. Rabbit, however, has great difficulty with Tigger's spontaneity and "bounciness." Rabbit is an introvert. He needs a lot of alone time, and when visitors come to his door he may pretend he isn't home. Rabbit is also an organizer *par excellence*. In fact, not content with organizing his own life, he tries to organize the life of everyone he knows. When Rabbit finds he is not able to organize Tigger, he decides to "unbounce" him. " 'There's too much of him,' said Rabbit, 'that's what it comes to.' " [1]

So Rabbit takes the unsuspecting Tigger on a "long explore," with the goal of getting him lost. Rabbit anticipates that after a night alone in the forest, Tigger will be "a different Tigger altogether"—humble, sad, melancholy, and definitely bounceless. [2] Once Rabbit explains that this will be for Tigger's own good, Pooh and Piglet join the scheme.

The plan starts well. The three conspirators take Tigger into the woods, wait until he has bounced out of sight, and then hide. Tigger searches vainly for his friends and then goes home to dinner. The others, however, can't find their own way home. Rabbit will not admit they are lost, and the others follow him in circles for many hours. Finally, Pooh and Piglet realize the reality of their situation, and Pooh "tunes in" to his inner guiding wisdom. He tells Piglet, "There are twelve pots of honey in my cupboard, and they've been calling to me for hours. I couldn't hear them properly before, because Rabbit *would* talk, but if nobody says anything except those twelve pots, I *think*, Piglet, I shall know where they're calling from." [3] And the two friends follow the call to their home.

The next morning, Tigger becomes concerned when he discovers that Rabbit is missing. He begins "tearing around the Forest making loud yapping noises for Rabbit." And at last "a very Small and Sorry Rabbit" hears him. And the "Small and Sorry Rabbit rushed through the mist at the noise, and it suddenly turned into Tigger: a Friendly Tigger, a Grand Tigger, a Large and Helpful Tigger, a Tigger who bounced ... in just the beautiful way a Tigger ought to bounce. " 'Oh, Tigger, I am glad to see you,' cried Rabbit." [4]

It is a deep truth that when we try to change others against their will, we will lose our own grounding, our center, and our spiritual way.

Spiritual Role Models

Flora Slosson Wuellner (1928–)

We are to search with passion for our deepest longing—our inner, burning power to love as we grow within God's heart. And, when we have found the great gift for which we came into the world, we are to let nothing interfere with its unfolding and release.

Flora has had a ministry of individual and communal spiritual renewal and inner healing for fifty-five years. She is an international teacher, retreat leader, spiritual director, and author of thirteen books. Flora is an ordained minister in the United Church of Christ.

Two of her books are *Forgiveness, The Passionate Journey* and *Enter by the Gate.* Flora's first book, *Prayer, Stress and Our Inner Wounds,* is still selling well after twenty-three years.

As a young teen, Flora was a "total introvert." Later, Flora felt that God was inviting her to move out of her shell of shyness. She calls this "a radical change."

As Flora answered the call to ordered minisry, she was much more comfortable acting in an extrovertd way. "When with others as pastor, I pushed myself into the exuberant 'Tigger' model, thinking that was the appropriate stance as a leader. . . . Obviously there was . . . a certain amount of inner conflict about complete self-acceptance."

It took years for Flora to find her true balance. Now she views herself as an omnivert with a strong introvert leaning. The extrovert energy she experiences during workshops and retreats is a "wonderful temporary rush. . . . I believe that God challenges us to explore the other orientation. . . . I always offer options for individual and small-group activities. Then extroverts and introverts can choose the activities they sense God calling them to."

You introverts may find that some of the following tips ask you to try new attitudes and behaviors. I believe that incorporating these tips into your way of being with extroverts will help both of you on your spiritual path.

Affirm Actively

I hope that by this point in the book you realize that extrovert spirituality is as beautiful and wonderful as introvert spirituality. If you do, please tell the extroverts you know. Many extroverts told me that active affirmation of their extroversion was the most helpful thing another person could do for them.

Some introverts believe they are being supportive by showing nonverbal acceptance of the extrovert. But extroverts are used to responding verbally to experiences that interest them, and if the introvert never speaks, the extrovert may either think the introvert doesn't understand or is judging them. This doesn't mean that the introvert needs to continually affirm the extrovert; one or two statements of acceptance and understanding will be remembered and cherished.

The results of a research study by Dr. Avril Thorne has some bearing on this issue. In studying a group of college students, she found that after an extrovert and introvert pair finished a conversation, each had shifted slightly to become closer to the other's orientation. [5]

I presume that each pair of students in the study felt somewhat equal in terms of power. It might be fascinating to have a similar study involving pairs of unequal power in conversation, such as a student and a teacher, a counselor and a client, a spiritual accompanier and a spiritual seeker. Even though the authority figure might not consciously be exercising power over the other, the relationship could be subtly affected, since the one being helped may feel admiration and respect and may strive to be like the helper.

Even though, as a psychologist, I know of this tendency involving relationships with authority figures, I sometimes find myself imitating the mannerisms, speech patterns, or preferences of those people whose spirituality I admire. I have been fortunate that these people, mostly introverts, have told me in clear terms that my extroversion is valid, although it may be different from their own spiritual style.

In most of my presentations over the past year, I mentioned that I was conducting a study of extrovert spirituality. Quite a few folk approached me after presentations and said something like, "It seems that many of the extroverts I see for spiritual accompaniment become more introverted over the span of our relationship. I wonder what's going on?" When I ask, "Do you acknowledge their extroversion and affirm it verbally?" the response is usually, "No, I've never thought to do that."

One reason the extroverted spiritual seekers may be acting more introverted over time is because, on a conscious or subconscious level, they receive the message that an introverted style is more spiritually valid. Whether you're a family member, a friend, or someone supporting others' spirituality in a lay or professional capacity, affirming the spirituality of extroverts in an active and verbal way will be a great blessing to them.

Share Your Own Journey

Differences can be seen as part of life's harmony if they are acknowledged and at least somewhat understood. I say "somewhat" because I can never fully know what it is like to be you. After all, it is difficult enough to understand myself!

An extrovert spoke out at a workshop I gave recently, saying, "I don't know why silent retreats are so popular. Why spend all that time, energy, and money being bored?" When I asked the woman if she had ever talked with someone who enjoyed them, she responded, "You mean, some people actually like them? I thought they were some sort of spiritual endurance test!" After lunch that day, the woman asked to speak to the group again. "Well, have I had my eyes opened! Three people asked to have lunch with me. I heard a number of stories about how wonderful silent retreats are for them. I still don't think that's a spiritual practice I will embrace, but now I can believe its helpful and even deeply satisfying for some."

Hope, a cloistered nun and an introvert, talks to people about their spiritual paths while they are on retreat at her monastery. Hope has discovered that extroverts often need to know more about her or they will misunderstand her motives. She wrote:

The first challenge for me when directing extroverts is to listen attentively to the overwhelming amount of "story" that unfolds before me. I remember quite vividly the first time I met with a high extrovert. The person began with great gusto and enthusiasm to share her story, which was filled with varied emotions and complex situations. We kept good eye contact, but when she finished I simply sat still, in silence. I had been stunned by her outburst and was gathering my thoughts.

Suddenly I noticed anxiety on my companion's face and a little panic in her eyes. I asked, "Are you okay?" She looked quizzically at me and said, "Well, aren't you going to respond to what I have shared?" I immediately laughed and said, "Of course, I am, but it's going to take me a moment to figure out where to start!" We were able to talk about our differences, and I explained that when I was silent there was no judgment attached; I was simply absorbing what I had learned, and I needed time to respond.

As in any other sphere of life, it is easy to judge self or others out of ignorance or unfamiliarity. Very few of the folks in my study received any education about extroverts' spiritual needs in theological colleges or spiritual-direction training programs. Anna, who lives in Arequipa, Peru, but was educated in the United States, wrote that in her training it was suggested she look at the Myers-Briggs Scale, Enneagram, and Jungian psychology on her own. She was given no information about the differences and similarities between extroverts and introverts. "I realize that sharing one's spiritual journey is much easier for us extroverts than for you introverts. We don't need to hear all the details of your spiritual experiences." But it does help both you and me if you help me to understand some of our different ways of being in the world.

Listen Intelligently

Intelligent listening takes the other person's characteristics into account. It doesn't get lost in all the details that extroverts tend to give. It doesn't become confused when seemingly unrelated topics are introduced. It demonstrates understanding so that listener and speaker can communicate effectively.

Mardi Tindal is a busy extrovert! She has worked as an educator, award-winning video producer, broadcaster, and writer. Currently she is executive director of Five Oaks Centre, an education and retreat center affiliated with the United Church of Canada. She is author of Soul Maps: A Guide to the Mid Life Spirit, which was made into an international award-winning documentary. Mardi wrote, "Being listened to in a holy way is extremely helpful to me. I am able to talk through all kinds of things and then have my spiritual guide help me to hear what I'm saying in God's terms. It helps me to be engaged in spiritual practice in my own extroverted way."

To listen intelligently to extroverts, introverts need to develop strategies to keep themselves from being overwhelmed. Dodie Huff-Fletcher, a Baptist and introverted spiritual director from Kentucky, found a way to deal with this issue.

I had been working for six months with one woman who was an extrovert, and I found myself not wanting to attend the sessions when she was scheduled. I would review my day ahead and sigh when I saw her name. I secretly hoped that she would call and cancel, and I considered whether or not to call her and cancel.

I took this concern to supervision and to prayer, and I realized that what was going on was a result of her extroversion and my introversion, combined with my desire to meet her need for drawing energy from others. She would come into a session tired and would leave invigorated, while I would come into the session feeling energized and leave feeling drained.

After that, I began making time before my sessions with extroverts to center and pray. As a result, I found that I was able to stay energized throughout the session, while at the same time my extroverted directee was also able to leave energized.

I no longer dread sessions with my extroverted directees, but find them stimulating.

Whether you're an introvert or an extrovert, it is probably not possible to remember every detail of what an extrovert tells you. Even if it were, it would not be helpful. Extroverts are more concerned that you get the gist, the essential point or meaning of the story. Introverted friends of extroverts tell me that it seems to work best when they simply let the words flow, trusting that out of the river of words the important things will bob to the surface. Trying to dam or divert the river is exhausting and unproductive.

A few years ago, Shirley Wilson of New Zealand did some very interesting research on spiritual directors' perceptions of extroverts. From her results, she concluded that extroverts need to be encouraged to speak in the way that is normal for them. She believes "an essential spiritual work for extroverts is 'coming into a healthy place' in relation to their outer lives, in particular their relationships. This may have the extrovert moving rapidly across the landscape of their lives, but it does not necessarily mean the directee is unfocused. Indeed the directee may be very focused." [6] Shirley suggests that those who wish to listen intelligently to extroverts respond in ways that deepen the extroverts' stories rather than trying to keep the speaker to a narrow topic.

To use our previous metaphor, intelligent listening will help the extrovert swim successfully in their river of words and will help the introvert listener stay calm, cool, and collected on the shore.

Accept Extrovert Energy

Extroverts bring lots of energy to any contact. Experiencing this energy can be a delight for some. Christine Bannan of Auckland, New Zealand, wrote that talking with extroverts about their spirituality "can be very noisy and lots of fun for me." But, as we have seen earlier in this chapter, extrovert energy can overwhelm others.

Accepting extrovert energy does not mean letting yourself be overcome. Here are some tips for dealing effectively with that energy. These are intended for times when extroverts want to talk with you about their spirituality, but you may find the tips helpful whenever you interact with extroverts.

- Try praying or practicing other grounding techniques prior to contact with an extrovert.
- If possible, start the contact with a few moments of silence. If extroverts don't understand the reason for this silence, they may become bored or anxious.
- Be honest with the extrovert about your own energy capacity. Set time limits on the contact if necessary. Some extroverts may not understand, but hopefully they will respect your needs.
- Stop the extrovert periodically to give yourself an opportunity to catch up emotionally. Tanya is an introverted spiritual director from the United States. She spoke of learning, in supervision, how to accept the energy of a particularly extroverted client without going past her own boundaries: "My determination to stop the directee at significant junctures to seek clarity or to invite further exploration afforded me needed respite in remaining present to manageable portions of his process of thinking out loud."
- Take breaks. When an introvert friend and I spend a day together, she is firm about having some alone time in the middle of our contact. I have learned to enjoy the time for napping or settling down with a good book. I know she needs the time apart more than I do.

Be Yourself

This last tip may sound obvious. Some of the extroverts in my study, however, wrote that introvert friends would sometimes try to be more extroverted in their presence. Although I encourage introverts to cultivate extrovert energy, there is a difference between that intentional growth and pushing past personal limits in an attempt to please someone else.

From Tucson, Arizona, introverted spiritual director Teresa Blythe wrote, "Sometimes I have to make sure that I don't try to mirror the extrovert's energy level and conversation pace. I have to remember that they may have chosen me because I am different from them. Also I find that extroverts sometimes try to pull me into more casual conversation or a teaching role, and I have to be aware of staying in the special role of spiritual director."

Introversion is also a beautiful and wonderful thing. But extroverts will only realize that if you are living your true self.

Discussion or Journal Questions

For Introverts

1. Are there any changes you will make in how you interact with extroverts after reading this chapter? What are they, and how do you plan on making them?

2. Which of these tips are you already using, and how do extroverts respond to them?

For Extroverts

1. Has an introvert supported your spirituality? How have they done this? How did it make you feel?

2. Of the tips in this chapter, which would be most important for introverts to keep in mind when they are interacting with you?

14
Maturing Extrovert Spirituality

For it was you who formed my inward parts;
you knit me together in my mother's womb.
I praise you, for I am fearfully and wonderfully made.
—Psalm 139:13-14

In previous chapters, we have discussed what healthy extrovert spirituality looks like and have explored some of the challenges we extroverts face, including attitudes and behaviors that will help us transform those challenges into spiritual and psychological growth. In this chapter, the focus is on suggestions for living more fully into our spirituality.

Fluid Extroversion

Looking back over your life, how have you experienced your extroversion? Has it been static, or is it fluid? Many extroverts find that once they undertake an intentional journey of spiritual and psychological growth, their extroversion develops a fluidity. They become more or less extroverted over the years. Sometimes, upon further reflection, they realize that the ebb and flow of their extroversion in the past may have been geared to meet the needs of their changing lives. How wonderful that we can become what will help us most!

Here's a story that was told to me by an extrovert in one of my workshops:

I had some major surgery that necessitated six weeks of bed rest. What worried me most, prior to surgery, wasn't the pain. I thought the inactivity would drive me up the wall. I'm such an active person. And I wouldn't see other people nearly as much, since my friends worked days. Once I had recovered enough physically to be sent home from the hospital, I did become really bored and irritable. Everybody heard how bad it was for me. I even complained to God.

Well, God did something about it! One day, I was saying a prayer of gratitude for everyone who was helping me, and instead of finishing within a few minutes, as I usually did, I found myself being drawn down to a deep inner place where I was resting in waves of comfort. When I came out of the prayer, nearly an hour had gone by, and I felt very peaceful and refreshed. That "drawing down" happened frequently during my convalescence. I definitely became more introverted. I was able to lie quietly and just let my mind rest, even when I wasn't in prayer.

I wondered what it would be like after I recovered. Well, I've gone back to being the extrovert I was before, although sometimes I will consciously focus inward and be fed by the energy I had discovered when I was recuperating.

As this story shows, God can help us shift along the extrovert-introvert continuum. However, it needs to be with our agreement; our Creator is passionate about our free will!

Balancing Extrovert and Introvert Practices

Once we say yes to a more fluid extroversion, we can do our part in our spiritual growth by cultivating meaningful spiritual practices. I believe that at any one time, no matter how extroverted or introverted we normally are, it is beneficial to find a balance between the two types of practice.

Spiritual Directors

Mary Elizabeth Nono

Mary Elizabeth Nono divides her time between Cheshire in the Northwest of the United Kingdom and the Isle of Anglesey in North Wales. She is lay, Catholic, single, and an extrovert. During 1993, 1994, and 1995 she trained to accompany others on their spiritual journey.

Currently she facilitates Quiet Days and Prayer Weeks, gives the full Spiritual Exercises of St. Ignatius, and provides ongoing spiritual direction. She organizes training courses in spiritual direction with the ecumenical Salford Prayer Guides. At present she serves as an elected member of the executive of the Catholic Network for Retreats and Spirituality, a constituent body of the UK Retreat Association. She is very involved with the Altrincham interfaith group.

"In reading your rsearch results, as an extrovert, all I can say is, 'Wow!' I felt so in tune with them. I have experienced professional helpers judging my extroverted spirituality as being too loud and have heard the extroverts who come to me express the same concern.

In my own spiritual journey, I am aware of becoming more and less extroverted at different times, and I will now call myself an omnivert. I agree with you that this is the trend for a number of spiritual seekers—those who begin as extroverts or introverts."

A balance point, however, is not a static, rigid position. Imagine yourself for a moment to be sitting on a large exercise ball. You will find that you need to be moving almost continually, making tiny adjustments, in order to stay on it. The movements may seem small, but without them you could not keep your balance.

Spiritual Role Models

Lois Miriam Wilson (1927–)

*Many think of religion as dogma. I think of it as an engagement
with the holy and with others.*

Ordained a United Church minister in 1965, The Very
Rev the Hon Lois M. Wilson shared team congregational
ministry for fifteen years with her husband the Reverend Dr.
Roy Wilson before becoming the first woman moderator of
the United Church of Canada. She was president of both the
Canadian Council of Churches and World Council of
Churches. Known as a leading advocate of interfaith en-
counters within Canada and of international human rights,
she has served as a board member of the Canadian Institute
for International Peace and Security, chair of the Board of
Rights and Democracy, and officer with the Ontario Human
Rights Commission. She has authored seven books and has
served as chancellor of Lakehead University.

Lois Wilson served a four-year appointment as a member of
the Refugee Status Advisory Committee and an eight-year ap-
pointment as a panel member of the Environmental Assess-
ment Review Board for the Disposal of Nuclear Waste in
Canada. As independent senator in Canada in 1998, she was
Canada's special envoy to the Sudan, led Government dele-
gations to China and North Korea, and cofounded the Senate
Standing Committee on Human Rights. She cochaired the
Canadian Committee on Women, Peace, and Security for the
United Nations and was awarded the World Federalist Peace
Prize and United Nations (Canada) Pearson Peace Medal.
And currently, she is the Ecumenist in Residence at the
Toronto School of Theology, U of T, offering public forums
on Religion and Public Policy.

Life is like that exercise ball. We constantly need to adjust to our present reality by choosing spiritual practices that are appropriate to that reality and therefore that lead to more freedom, healing, and love.

This does not mean picking up and dropping spiritual practices every day or two. As we have seen, any spiritual practice can be done in an extroverted or introverted way. Our practices will adjust as needed if we cultivate flexibility.

Becoming Omniverts

When I began to study extrovert spirituality, I thought most people would fall neatly into E or I categories. My research surprised me, showing that many extroverts are able to move to an introvert place when needed. This ability usually seemed to come about through conscious decision and subsequent practice, or through divine invitation and subsequent practice.

Some of my respondents seemed to move past fluid extroversion—that is, instead of just shifting up and down the extrovert-introvert continuum, they were able to be energized by both outer and inner energy during any one point in their lives. I don't know if we can be energized in both ways at the same time; I do know of a number of people who draw on each type of energy at various times in their day. For example, Cynthie begins her day with the extroverted practice of singing and dancing praise to music. Then, after she eats her lunch and chats with her coworkers, she takes fifteen minutes for introverted centering prayer.

Cynthie is an omnivert. Frank is also an omnivert, although he says he tends not to do much "looking inside" and so had not been aware of his orientation until he participated in my study. He wrote, "During over fifty years working as a teacher, parish priest, and member of a retreat team, I did not look at my ministry as 'extrovert' or 'introvert.' Now, in hindsight, I would say that I am mostly extrovert in my ministry with people and am mostly introvert in my personal life and study times."

Even though they and I didn't initially have a name for it, I believe a number of my respondents are omniverts. I think there are spiritual and psychological benefits to becoming omniverts, or at least to being extroverts with some introvert practices. In a previous chapter we talked about the danger of becoming slaves to our need for stimulation. It can also mean using less of our potential.

Recall for a moment the research that showed increased blood flow for the extroverts in the rear of their brains and increased flow for the introverts in the front of their brains. If we only cultivate extroverted spiritual practices, we will only be able to respond to life partially. Learning to activate both parts of our brain allows us many more options for meeting our spiritual and psychological needs. We become more flexible and can find meaning and joy in many different types of spirituality.

Final Words

For the past two days I have been giving a workshop titled Spiritual Renovations, which is designed to help people be more sensitive to divine guidance during life's challenging times. One-third of the group were extroverts. As the group shared stories about times of stress and loss in their lives, one introverted Catholic nun told us about a different type of prayer God invited her into many years previously. "When I feel God's presence, I respond with love," she said. "But ever since I told my spiritual director, he has been trying to get me to stay with the traditional contemplative prayer."

What a wonderful lead-in to a discussion of extroverted and introverted spiritual practices! Many people in the group decided they were omniverts, and others had great fun comparing their extrovert or introvert spirituality. I was delighted to see people understanding their spiritual needs and feeling free to show their true spiritual face to the world.

Please let me know how this book has touched your life; you may contact me at reeves@nancyreeves.com. And may you find that your spiritual path helps you become the person you know you can be. Blessings to you.

Activity

Extroversion Through Your Lifetime

Has your experience of extroversion changed over the years? Using the descriptors listed below, describe your extroversion at different points in your lifetime. You may wish to describe an incident that illustrates each time period.

If you find that your extroversion has changed at times, move more deeply into your memory and see if you can discover how the changes came about. Can you discover God's presence in the invitation to change or the ability to change? How did the changes help you at that time in your life?

	Very E	Somewhat E	Balanced E & I	Somewhat I	Very I	Omnivert
Early childhood						
Older childhood						
Teen years						
Early adulthood						
Middle adult years						
Elder adult years						

Discussion or Journal Questions

1. Do you believe it is beneficial to develop both extroverted and introverted spiritual practices? Please explain your answer.

2. Do you know any omniverts? Are you one? What do you think of the concept of omniverts?

USING THIS BOOK
IN GROUPS

Are you attracted to the idea of exploring extrovert spirituality with others? Put up a poster or make a request in the church bulletin, and you may find yourself with a group of other interested people. The material in this section is designed to help you use this book in group settings.

Groups can consist of both extroverts and introverts, which should serve to encourage understanding between the two orientations. At various points in the book I have included questions for introverts, and extroverts may benefit from hearing the answers.

You may find that people wish the group to consist solely of extroverts or introverts, which is fine. I have had a number of requests already for an extrovert retreat, where people can try some of the extroverted and introverted spiritual practices described in this book. Although introverts may not be attracted to groups with the same intensity or frequency as extroverts, you may find that there is enough interest to form an introvert group on this topic.

Types of Groups

In this section I describe several different types of groups you may want to consider forming. Whichever type you select, you'll find that the topic of extrovert spirituality is of interest to seekers who are not connected to a faith tradition. If you advertise the group in local papers, you may attract seekers who were negatively judged regarding their spirituality and therefore left a particular congregation. If you do open the group, be aware that beginning and ending with a prayer, especially a Christian one, may initially evoke anxiety. Instead it may be good to say something short, such as "May each of us be open to the words that will help us to become freer, more loving people."

133

Study Group

For study groups I suggest eight sessions, each lasting forty-five minutes to an hour. Each session can cover one chapter, with the chapters on specific spiritual practices being divided between two sessions. If group members read the chapters ahead of time, there will be more time for discussion. If members prefer to be introduced to the material in the group, half of the session can be spent in presentation and half in discussion.

Daylong Workshop

For daylong workshops I suggest presenting each topic briefly, with perhaps one story from the book, to illustrate each of the points made. Participants will appreciate time to discuss, reflect quietly, and complete some of the activities suggested at the end of chapters. Try to structure the workshop to accommodate both extroverts and introverts. For example, when I send workshop participants off to do a thirty-minute activity on their own, I will usually say, "If you prefer to stay away until we begin the next topic, please return in thirty minutes. If you would like to discuss this activity in a small group, return in fifteen minutes."

Weekend Retreat

This will be a slower-paced format than the workshop. More personal exploration and prayer time can be included. Retreat participants can be given opportunities to practice a number of extroverted and introverted spiritual practices.

Weeklong Summer Camp

Over five days, participants will be able to experience and appreciate each topic being presented at greater length, with perhaps one story from the book to illustrate each of the points made. I suggest that you spend two-thirds of each session on activities and discussion—especially if there are lots of extroverts in the group!

Forming a Group

You will need at least one person to advertise, organize, and co-ordinate the group. This person also may serve as the group facilitator. The facilitator should be present at each group session to welcome members, keep time, and help people stay on track. It will help promote a feeling of safety and trust to have some group rules that are agreeable to all.

During the first session, decide which rules the group wishes to use. Write them on a flip chart and post them each week as a reminder. Here are some suggested group rules:

- The group will begin and end on time.
- Share briefly. Everyone deserves time to speak.
- Group members choose their own level of participation. Silence is fine. No one should be pressured to share.
- Confidentiality: Everything shared in the group stays in the group.
- Anonymity: Members' identities are not to be shared outside.
- No advice giving. Don't tell fellow group members what they should or should not do.
- No judgments. All group members are entitled to their own opinions.
- This is an educational group intended to discuss spiritual and psychological material. It is not a counseling or psychotherapy group.

Tips for the Facilitator

Many people have never shared details of their spiritual life, or they may have received judgment in the past when they did share. Reassure participants by explaining the primary benefit of this kind of sharing, which is that group members may become spiritual friends who support, encourage, and guide one another as they explore the topic and deepen their faith. Watch, though, that members do not share too intimately. Some people may get caught up in the accepting atmosphere of the group and later regret that they shared so deeply. If someone begins a story that seems unusually personal, you may want to gently stop them.

You are a member of the group as well. Keep in mind, however, that some members will give your comments more weight because they see you as being in charge. So after sharing your own stories and thoughts, bring the focus back to the other members by saying something such as, "Now, does anyone else have something they want to say?" Otherwise, members may begin looking to you always to lead the discussion.

Although there may be many diverse ideas in the group, you will need to stop any words that are racist, sexist, slandering, blaming, shaming, or unnecessarily negative. It is easier to do this if you have established a group rule specifying that all group members are entitled to their own opinions and that judgmental comments are not welcome.

SUGGESTED READING

(Some Books and CDs by Extroverts and Extrovert-Friendly Authors)

Au, Wilkie and Noreen Cannon Au. *By Way of the Heart: Towards a Holistic Christian Spirituality*. Mahwah, N.J.: Paulist Press, 1990.

———. *The Discerning Heart: Exploring the Christian Path*. Mahwah, N.J.: Paulist Press, 2006.

———. *The Enduring Heart: Spirituality for the Long Haul*. Mahwah, N.J.: Paulist Press, 2005.

Borysenko, Joan. *Inner Peace for Busy People*. Carlsbad, Calif.: Hay House, 2001.

———. *Saying Yes to Change*. Carlsbad, Calif.: Hay House, 2005.

———. *The Ways of the Mystic: Seven Paths to God*. Carlsbad, Calif.: Hay House, 1997.

Brown, Patricia. *Paths to Prayer*. San Francisco: Jossey-Bass, 2003.

De Chardin, Pierre Teilhard. *The Heart of the Matter*. New York: Harvest Books, 2002.

———. *Le Milieu Divin*. London: Collins, 1957.

Finley, Kathleen. *The Liturgy of Motherhood: Moments of Grace*. Lanham, Md.: Sheed and Ward, 2004.

———. *Prayers for the Newly Married*. Skokie, Ill.: ACTA Publications, 2006.

———. *Savoring God: Praying with All Our Senses*. Notre Dame: Ave Maria Press, 2003.

———. *Welcome! Prayers for New and Pregnant Parents*. Liguori, Mo.: Liguori Press, 2004.

Good, Linnea. *The Greatest of These: The Best of Good*. (CD, 2007) www.linneagood.com.

———. *Swimmin' Like a Bird* (CD, 2005) www.linneagood.com.

Harding, Bruce and Cheryl Harding. *Like a Healing Stream* (CD, 2003) www.evensong.ca.

———. *This Is the Day* (CD, 2006) www.evensong.ca.

Hawker, Paul. *Secret Affairs of the Soul*. Kelowna: Northstone, 2000.

———. *Soul Quest: A Spiritual Odyssey Through 40 Days & 40 Nights of Mountain Solitude*. Kelowna: Northstone, 2007.

Hays, Edward. *Pray All Ways*. Notre Dame, Ind.: Ave Maria Press, 2007.

———. *Prayers for the Domestic Church*. Notre Dame, Ind.: Ave Maria Press, 2007.

———. *Prayers for a Planetary Pilgrim*. Notre Dame, Ind.: Ave Maria Press, 1988.

Jones, W. Paul. *An Eclectic Almanac for the Faithful: People, Places, and Events That Shape Us*. Nashville: Upper Room Books, 2006.

———. *A Table in the Desert: Making Space Holy*. Orleans, Mass.: Paraclete Press, 2001.

———. *Teaching the Dead Bird to Sing : Living the Hermit Life Within*. Orleans, Mass.: Paraclete Press, 2002

Morgan, Richard L. *With Faces to the Evening Sun*. Nashville: Upper Room Books, 1998.

————. *Fire in the Soul: A Prayer Book for the Later Years*. Nashville: Upper Room Books, 2000.

————. *Settling In: My First Year in a Retirement Community*. Nashville: Upper Room Books, 2007.

Oliva, Max. *Free to Pray, Free to Love: Growing in Prayer & Compassion*. Notre Dame, Ind.: Ave Maria Press, 1994.

————. *God of Many Loves*. Notre Dame, Ind.: Ave Maria Press, 2001.

————. *The Masculine Spirit: Resources for Reflective Living*. Notre Dame, Ind.: Ave Maria Press, 1997.

Pritchard, Sheila. *The Lost Art of Meditation: Deepening Your Prayer Life*. Bletchley, U.K.: Scripture Union, 2003.

Reeves, Nancy. *Adventures of the God Detectives*. Kelowna, B.C.: Wood Lake Books, 2006.

————. *Found Through Loss*. Kelowna: Northstone, 2003.

————. *I'd Say Yes God, If I Knew What You Wanted*. Kelowna: Northstone, 2001.

————. *A Match Made in Heaven: A Bible-based Guide to Deepening Your Relationship with God*. Nashville: Abingdon Press, 2007.

————. *The Midwife's Story: Meditations for Advent Times*. Illustrations by Margaret Kyle. Kelowna: Northstone, 2003.

————. *A Path Through Loss: A Guide to Writing Your Healing and Growth*. Kelowna: Northstone, 2001.

Rohr, Richard. *Everything Belongs: The Gift of Contemplative Prayer*. Crossroad Publishing, 2003.

Rohr, Richard and friends. *Contemplation in Action*. New York: Crossroad Publishing, 2006.

Rohr, Richard with John Brookser Feister. *Hope Against Darkness: The Transforming Vision of Saint Francis in an Age of Anxiety*. Cincinnati: St. Anthony Messenger Press, 2001.

Rupp, Joyce. *The Cosmic Dance: An Invitation to Experience Our Oneness*. Maryknoll, N.Y.: Orbis Books, 2002.

———. *The Cup of Our Life: A Guide for Spiritual Growth*. Notre Dame, Ind.: Ave Maria Press, 1997.

Rupp, Joyce and Macrina Wiederkehr. *The Circle of Life: The Heart's Journey Through the Seasons*. Notre Dame, Ind.: Sorin Books, 2005.

Wilson, Lois. *Miriam, Mary, and Me*. Kelowna: Northstone, 1996.

———. *Turning the World Upside Down: A Memoir*. Toronto: Doubleday, 1989.

RESEARCH ON EXTROVERSION

Psychological Research

Myers-Briggs Type Indicator

Carl Jung coined the terms *extrovert* and *introvert* as part of a larger psychological type theory. Prior to the 1923 publication of Jung's book *Psychological Types*, Katherine Briggs had also been working on personality types. Later extending Jung's theory with her own research, Briggs and her daughter, Isabel Briggs Myers, developed a test that categorizes people into one of sixteen types, using combinations of four "preferences" for functioning in the world: extroversion/introversion, sensing/intuition, thinking/feeling, and judging/perceiving.

The Myers-Briggs Type Indicator has been widely used and researched in settings such as education, the workplace, prisons, and religious and spiritual groups and institutions. Numerous books have been written on the Myers-Briggs material. In their own book, *Gifts Differing*, the authors comment on extroverts, saying that the extrovert tends to be "more open, accessible, communicative, and friendly" than the introvert. [1] "Well-developed extroverts can deal effectively with ideas, but they do their best work externally, in action." [2]

Extroversion in Other Theories

Frequently, psychological and spiritual researchers use test materials based on the research of Hans Eysenck. In his 1947 book *Dimensions of Personality*, he identified extroversion somewhat differently from the definition used by Jung. He described it as the tendency to enjoy positive events, particularly if the events are social. He developed a number of test materials, including the Eysenck Personality Inventory.

Some folk become aware of extroversion through the Enneagram, a psychological tool that describes people as being one of nine personality types, based on their motivations.

Biological Research

Debra Johnson and some colleagues published an article in the February 1999 issue of *The American Journal of Psychiatry*. [3] The researchers used positron emission tomography (PET) to examine brain activity in extroverts and introverts, measuring cerebral blood flow. While participants were being scanned, all they were told to do was to relax and let their thoughts go where they would.

Findings indicated that during free-flowing thought, different parts of the brain showed more activity in extroverts and introverts. The extroverts experienced more brain activity in the posterior thalamus and posterior insula. These areas are involved in interpreting sensory data.

The introverts had increased activity in the frontal lobes, the anterior thalamus, and other structures which are associated with problem-solving, making plans, and memory. One might say, therefore, that both groups ran true to type: the extroverts' focus was more outward, and the introverts' focus was more inward.

In June 2002, the journal *Science* published an article titled "Amygdala Response to Happy Faces as a Function of Extroversion." Psychology professor Dr. Turhan Canli and colleagues conducted research on the amygdala, a pea-sized area of the brain in the middle of the head, behind the ears. The amygdala is associated with memory and emotion, and many studies show that it becomes aroused when a person views fearful faces. Researchers found split results, however, when happy faces were viewed.

Dr. Canli and his colleagues wondered if the differing results were due to differences in extroversion and introversion. In their study, they indeed found that the more extroverted the participant, the more the amygdala was affected. [4] Many studies have shown that people seek out experiences that stimulate their brains. So it appears likely that an extrovert would respond more positively to a happy face than would a more introverted person.

Other Research on Spiritual Extroverts

Shirley Wilson, a spiritual director in New Zealand, conducted research on extroverts as part of her spiritual-direction training program at Spiritual Growth Ministries. She wrote an article describing her results, titled "Offering Spiritual Direction to Extroverts," which can be found online at www.sgm.org.nz.

The article contains much valuable information. Shirley interviewed twenty-three spiritual directors and focused on the following issues:

- Since extroverts do not usually prefer introspection, there is a popular belief that they would hesitate to seek out spiritual direction. Is this true?
- Do spiritual directors find it demanding to accompany extroverts? Specifically, is it difficult to keep the extrovert on track, to deal with the great amount of verbiage, and to cope with the energy demands involved in working with extroverts?
- Do extroverts respond well to some of the common techniques and approaches used by spiritual directors? [5]

Leslie J. Francis is professor of practical theology at the University of Wales in Bangor and Director of the Welsh National Centre for Religious Education. His main research interests include the study of personality and religion, the psychology of religion, clergy studies, and the relationship of religion and values.

Professor Francis is the author of a number of books and scores of studies that deal with extroversion. His most recent book is *Faith and Psychology: Personality, Religion and the Individual* (London: Darton, Longman and Todd, 2005).

I have included brief results from three of the studies that Professor Francis and his colleagues have undertaken. The first examined the growing interest in adult Christian education. His participants were twenty-nine men and thirty-two women attending a diocesan adult study program. They completed a questionnaire that asked for their attitudes toward the education program and also included an abbreviated form of the Revised Eysenck Personality Questionnaire. Results showed that extroverts were much more favorable toward this type of program than introverts were. [6]

The area of collaborative ministry was the focus of an article by Dr. Francis and his colleagues titled "Clergy Personality and Collaborative Ministry: The Way Ahead for Stable Extroverts?" [7] The article described a study in which the participants were 991 male clergy affiliated with the Evangelical Alliance in the United Kingdom. The study included the short-form Revised Eysenck Personality Questionnaire and a collaborative ministry scale. Extroverts by far preferred collaborative ministry.

Another article by Professor Francis and his colleagues, titled "Personality and Religion: Who Goes to Church for Fun?" describes a study dealing with the interest that extroverts have in outward stimulation. In the study, the researchers administered the abbreviated form of the Eysenck Personality Questionnaire to 923 churchgoers. The findings showed that an appreciation of fun and humor in worship is positively related to extroversion. [8]

REEVES RESEARCH

Email Text

Thank you for your willingness to take part in my research on extroverts and spiritual practices. If you would prefer a phone call or other, more direct, contact, please tell me. Just click "reply" to this email, add your answers at the end of each question, and send back.Your email address is acceptable as consent.

Peace,
Nancy

Consent Form

I consent to being a participant in this study about spiritual practices for extroverts. I understand that my participation in this research is completely voluntary and that I may decide freely to withdraw at any point in the research process.

I wish to remain anonymous and do not want any identifying information used in the research article or subsequent book. _____

I give permission for my name and identifying information to be used in the research article and subsequent book. _____

Note: There is no guarantee that a particular piece of information will be used in the research article or book.

Signature _____

Date _____

Address _____

Questionnaire

Extroverts: Complete A, B, and C
Extroverted spiritual directors or other spiritual accompaniers:
   Complete A-D
Introverted spiritual directors or other spiritual accompaniers:
   Complete A and D

A. Demographic Information

Age _____ Sex _____ Country in which you currently reside
_____

Religious affiliation (if any) _____

B. Extrovert Scale

   The following words are common descriptors for extroverts.
Please place a number beside each, to describe your current
experience.
1 = Never 2 = Rarely 3 = Sometimes 4 = Frequently 5 = Always

Outgoing _____
Comfortable in groups _____
Energized by being around people _____
Attention often directed outward _____
Like to be actively involved _____
Impulsive _____
Have a number of friends _____
Enjoy meeting new people _____

C. Questions for Extroverts

General instructions: Please answer each question briefly (1-3 sentences). You may then choose one or two to answer with a short story. (See sample short story at the end of the question-naire.) If a question is not applicable to you, please answer n/a, so that I will know you read and considered it.

1. At what age did you discover you were an extrovert?
2. How did you first discover you were an extrovert? (e.g. through a workshop)
3. Have you changed in how you think of "extroverts?" For ex-ample, did you ever judge extroverts as less spiritual, or more concerned with social justice than introverts?
4. Describe spiritual practices that are meaningful/helpful to you.
5. Describe spiritual practices that are not meaningful/helpful to you.
6. If you have been in a formal spiritual direction or other spir-itual accompaniment process, describe an experience in this process that helped or hindered your "extrovertedness."
7. Through your lifetime, have you become (a) more extro-verted, (b) less extroverted, (c) more or less at various times, (d) same, yet added some introverted spiritual practices?
8. How has your "extrovertedness" impacted on your spirituality?
9. For those that believe in a divine being, do you have a par-ticular image for or way of experiencing that being?
10. Do you have any spiritual role models who were or are extroverts?
11. Have you experienced divine guidance in a particularly ex-troverted way?
12. Has a particular book been helpful to you in understanding the spiritual needs of extroverts?
13. What was it like for you to participate in this study?
14. Is there an unasked question you wish to answer?

D. Questions for Spiritual "Accompaniers" (Extroverted and Introverted)

General instructions: Please answer each question briefly (1-3 sentences) and choose one or two to answer with a short story. (See sample short story at the end of the questionnaire) If a question is not applicable to you, please answer n/a, so that I will know you read and considered it.

1. What term would you use to describe your spiritual accompaniment? (e.g. spiritual direction, pastoral care, counseling)
2. What term would you use to describe your role? (e.g. pastor, counselor, spiritual director)
3. How long have you assisted others with their spirituality?
4. Describe your formal or informal spiritual accompaniment training. (e.g. MDiv through VST or informal training and supervision from a spiritual director in my religious order)
5. Has your training addressed the spiritual needs of extroverts?
6. Have you changed in how you think of "extroverts?" For example, did you ever judge extroverts as less spiritual or more concerned with social justice than introverts?
7. (For introverts) What are some of the challenges introverted spiritual accompaniers face in supporting extroverts on their spiritual path?
8. (For extroverts) What are some of the challenges extroverted spiritual directors face in accompanying extroverts on their spiritual path?
9. (For extroverts) What are some of the challenges extroverted spiritual directors face in accompanying introverts on their spiritual path?
10. Has a particular book been helpful to you in understanding the spiritual needs of extroverts?
11. What was it like for you to participate in this study?
12. Is there an unasked question you wish to answer?

Research Findings

I received seventy-one requests to participate in my research, "Spirituality for Extroverts." Fifty-eight returned completed questionnaires, which represented an eighty-two-percent return rate.

Fifty-one participants were extroverts, and seven were introverts who accompany extroverts on their spiritual path.

Participants in the study ranged in age from twenty-four to eighty-eight years of age. Over half were between fifty-four and sixty-seven. Seventy-six percent were female; 24 percent were male. Forty-four people (76 percent) who took part in my research were Christian. Six participants stated they did not have a particular faith tradition, three were Jewish, two Unitarian Universalist, one interfaith, one Taoist, and one who listed herself as a Spiritual Universalist.

Ninety-three percent of the respondents were North American. Twenty-nine lived in the United States, and twenty-five lived in Canada. Two participants lived in New Zealand, one in Australia, and one in Peru.

(1) Extrovert Scale Results

	Never	Rarely	Some-times	Frequently	Always
Outgoing			5	35	9
Comfortable in groups			4	31	15
Energized by being around people			5	23	23
Attention often directed outward			13	28	8
Like to be actively involved			10	29	11
Impulsive		5	28	16	3

	Never	Rarely	Some-times	Frequently	Always
Have a number of friends			9	21	24
Enjoy meeting new people			7	21	23

(2) When did you discover you were an extrovert?

Age discovered their extroversion	Number of participants
Childhood	7
Adolescence	11
20s	11
30s	7
40s	9
50s	3
70s	1

Extroversion over time

Experience of extroversion over time	Number of participants
More extroverted	7
Less extroverted	14
More or less at various times	20
Same, yet added some introverted spiritual practices	10

(3) What was it like for you to participate in this study?

All respondents answered this question. Twenty-five people said completing the questionnaire helped them grow in self-awareness.

For example, Diane wrote, "This was very important. . . . It helped me reflect on and claim my spiritual growth. Very helpful to articulate these thoughts. . . . I may even share this with my current spiritual director." An introverted spiritual director, Bill Peto, stated, "It awakened in me the awareness to bring this topic to our staff meeting for further discussion."

Sixteen participants wrote that completing the questionnaire was a very positive experience for them, and ten focused on how affirmed they felt. Jennifer stated, "Refreshing! Someone actually knows we're here!" Vanessa said, "It was a good exercise to put this down on paper, and I am happy to spread the good news that extroverts are spiritual too but in different ways." Bob wrote that responding to the questionnaire was all right, but "I would do much better if you were to have a group of us meet and talk about this. A questionnaire is really an introvert's tool. I need to get warmed up to share better."

(4) What training did you receive about extrovert spirituality?

None	No specifics	Marginal	Some	Yes, I did
8	12	4	4	7

(5) How have your extroversion and spirituality interacted?

Interaction of spirituality/ extroversion	Number of Participants
More comfortable around people	28
Enjoy a variety of spiritual experiences	12
Made spirituality more visible	7
Conscious relationship with God	6
Encouraged personal growth	5
Made me more judgmental about myself	4
Spiritual home	2

Made it more difficult to slow down   2
Can be seen as intimidating   1

(6) What are your most frequent spiritual practices?

Spiritual practice	Number of practitioners
Contemplative prayer and meditation	26
Singing and/or chanting	24
Sharing spiritual experiences with others	22
Prayer in movement	22
Group worship	21
Reading or watching movies for spiritual content	19
Being in nature	13
Spiritual writing or journaling	12

(7) What type of contemplative prayer do you practice?

Although sixteen respondents specifically mentioned that they did not find introverted contemplative prayer and meditation helpful, most did not describe the type of prayer that was helpful. Therefore, I emailed each of the twenty-six respondents who said they practiced contemplative prayer, asked them to describe the practice, and asked for specifics.

Type of contemplative prayer	Number of participants
Extrovert type	10
Introvert type	1
Both types	4
Did not indicate	11

NOTES

1. Are You a Tigger or an Owl?

1. E. D. Hirsch Jr., Joseph F. Kett, and James Trefil, eds., *New Dictionary of Cultural Literacy, 3rd ed.* (Boston: Houghton Mifflin, 2002).

2. Debra Johnson, et al., "Cerebral Blood Flow and Personality: A Positron Emission Tomography Study," *American Journal of Psychiatry,* vol. 156 (February 1999): 252-57.

3. Violet de Laszlo, ed., *The Basic Writings of C. G. Jung* (New York: Modern Library, 1959), 186.

2. Getting Extroverts Out of the Box

1. W. Paul Jones, "Extrovert Spirituality," *Leading from the Center* (Nashville: General Board of Discipleship, Summer 2002): 3.

2. James Brodrick, *Saint Francis Xavier* (New York: Wicklow Press, 1952), 33.

3. What Does Extrovert Spirituality Look Like?

1. Jose De Vinck, *Revelations of Women Mystics: From Middle Ages to Modern Times* (New York: Alba House, 1985), 163.

2. Ibid., 154. An English translation of Gabrielle's diary *He and I* is available from Evelyn M. Brown, Editions Pauline of Sherbrooke, Canada, 1969.]

3. David LaGesse, "Heeding Her Own Voice," *U.S. News* (October 10, 2005). See www.usnews.com/usnews/news/articles/051031/31winfrey.htm.

4. Nancy Reeves, *A Match Made in Heaven: A Bible-based Guide to Deepening Your Relationship with God* (Nashville: Dimensions for Living, 2007), 46.

4. A Few Words about Spiritual Practice

1. Patricia Brown, *Paths to Prayer: Finding Your Own Way to the Presence of God* (San Francisco: Jossey-Bass, 2003), 5.

5. Praying and Meditating

1. *A Book of Contemplation, the which is called The Cloud of Unknowing, in the which a Soul is Oned with God.* Edited from the British Museum MS. Harl. 674 with an introduction by Evelyn Underhill (London: J. M. Watkins, 1934), 33.

2. Ibid., 34, 50.
3. Thomas Keating, *Intimacy with God* (New York: Crossroad Publishing, 1994), 42.

6. Singing

1. Paul Hawker, *Soul Quest: A Spiritual Odyssey Through 40 Days & 40 Nights of Mountain Solitude* (Kelowna: Northstone, 2007), 131.
2. www.lrose.com

7. Cultivating Spiritual Friendships

1. Max Oliva, *God of Many Loves* (Notre Dame, Ind.: Ave Maria Press, 2001), 58.
2. Ibid., 59-60.

8. Moving Prayer

1. Sheila Pritchard, *The Lost Art of Meditation: Deepening Your Prayer Life* (Bletchley, U.K.: Scripture Union, 2003), 87.
2. Viki Hurst, *Personal Pilgrimage: One-day Soul Journeys for Busy People* (Kelowna: Northstone, 2000), 16.
3. Dalai Lama, *Freedom in Exile: The Autobiography of the Dalai Lama* (New York: Hodder & Stoughton, 1990), 44.
4. Ibid., 188.
5. Ibid., 201.

9. Practicing Spirituality in Groups

1. *AA Big Book* (New York: Alcoholics Anonymous, 2001), 76.

10. Spiritual Reading and Writing

1. www.catholic-forum.com.
2. Nancy Reeves, *I'd Say Yes God, If I Knew What You Wanted* (Kelowna: Northstone, 2001), 129.

11. Praying in Nature

1. Joyce Rupp and Macrina Wiederkehr, *The Circle of Life: The Heart's Journey Through the Seasons* (Notre Dame, Ind.: Sorin Books, 2005), 22.
2. Emily Dickinson, "No. 324," *The Poems of Emily Dickinson*, ed. R. W. Franklin (Cambridge, Mass.: Belknap Press, 1998), 106.

3. Patricia Barrett, *Sacred Garden: Soil for the Growing Soul* (Harrisburg, Pa.: Morehouse, 2000).

4. John Neihardt, *Black Elk Speaks: Being the Life Story of a Holy Man of the Oglala Sioux* (Lincoln, Neb.: University of Nebraska Press, 1932), 43.

5. www.kanuga.org/conferences/2007/photography.shtml.

6. Mary Lou Randour, *Animal Grace: Entering a Spiritual Relationship with Our Fellow Creatures* (Novato, Calif.: New World Library, 1999), 4.

7. Arthur Green, *Tormented Master: A Life of Rabbi Nahman of Bratslav* (New York: Shocken Books, 1981), 139.

12. Challenges of Being Extroverted Persons of Faith

1. Kathleen Finley, *Savoring God: Praying with All Our Senses* (Notre Dame, Ind.: Ave Maria Press, 2003), 12.

2. Bart D. Ehrman, *Peter, Paul, and Mary Magdalene* (New York: Oxford University Press, 2006), 21.

3. Marti Olsen Laney, *The Introvert Advantage: How to Survive in an Extrovert World* (New York: Workman, 2002).

13. Tips for Those Who Love Extroverts

1. A. A. Milne, *The World of Pooh* (Toronto: McClelland and Stewart, 1957), 253.

2. Ibid., 254.

3. Ibid., 265.

4. Ibid., 267.

5. Avril Thorne, "The Press of Personality: A Study of Conversations between Introverts and Extroverts," *Journal of Personality and Social Psychology*, vol. 53 (1987): 718-26.

6. Shirley Wilson, "Offering Spiritual Direction to Extroverts," *New Zealand Spiritual Growth Ministries* (www.sgm.org.nz).

Research on Extroversion

1. Isabel Briggs Myers with Peter B. Myers, *Gifts Differing* (Palo Alto, Calif.: Consulting Psychologists Press, 1980), 28.

2. Ibid., 8.

3. Debra Johnson, et al., "Cerebral Blood Flow and Personality: A Positron Emission Tomography Study," *American Journal of Psychiatry*, vol. 156 (February 1999): 252-57.

4. Turhan Canli, et al., "Amygdala Response to Happy Faces as a Function of Extraversion," *Science* (June 2002): 2191.

5. Shirley Wilson, "Offering Spiritual Direction to Extroverts," article on www.sgm.org.nz.

6. Leslie J. Francis, "Is Adult Christian Education Mainly for Stable Extraverts?" *Studies in the Education of Adults*, vol. 29 (1997): 191-99.

7. Leslie J. Francis, "Clergy Personality and Collaborative Ministry: The Way Ahead for Stable Extraverts?" *Pastoral Psychology*, vol. 53 (2004): 33-42.

8. Leslie J. Francis, "Personality and Religion: Who Goes to Church for Fun?" *Irish Journal of Psychology*, vol. 17 (1996): 71-74.